The Most Valuable Wedding Gift
A Guide to Partnership Finance
Through Money Conversations

Roderick M. Givens

MⓈM

Published by Marriage & Money LLC
Seattle

The Most Valuable Wedding Gift

A Guide to Partnership Finance Through Money Conversations

The Most Valuable Wedding Gift:
A Guide to Partnership Finance Through Money Conversations

ISBN 978-1-7347968-1-0 Softcover paperback
ISBN 978-1-7347968-0-3 E-book

In case you skipped the last page

DISCLAIMER

I don't know you - financially. This book does not provide <u>personalize</u> advice. Please use this as a <u>guide</u>, not exact step-by-step instructions regarding your personal situation. Proceed with caution with this and any other material related to your partnership decision-making.

Contents

Partnership Choices

It's Not Easy

Advanced

* Sections include situations that have been combined
and modified for efficiency and entertainment purposes.

Introduction

"TooooNiiiiiiiiiiiiiight"   The last notes of Donna Summer's disco classic "Last Dance," floats out over the dance floor. The DJ is starting to pack up. The venue staff has quietly begun to put away chairs and tables. Guests are gathering their belongings and saying their goodbyes.

The reception is over, but *your* journey is just beginning. You're married—and *Forever After* starts now. Regardless of how much time you've previously spent together, marriage is a new territory. You've joined the married club. You've moved from *I'm getting married* to *I'm married.* Congratulations! Now it's time to see what's behind the proverbial marriage curtain.

The goal of this book is to provide your partnership with insights to have better money conversations and, ultimately, make better decisions. Technically, this is a guide for partnerships to use their TEAM resources (Time, Energy, Ability, and Money) to have better conversations. Money conversations include both the "what to discuss" and "how to discuss" TEAM resources with an emphasis on money. We believe better conversations will 1) reduce stress caused by money, and 2) increase confidence leading to the partnership making better decisions. Better decisions should result in a better life when incorporating partnership resources, goals, and values with your human behaviors. That's a mouthful - so we'll just use the title *The Most Valuable Wedding Gift*.

Why money? Why now?

You might pause: "Whoa, we *just* got married. Can't we wait to talk about all this money stuff?" Although money conversations are meaningful, they seem less urgent until a problem arises. Many couples wait far too long to talk about strategic money decisions; often, the conversation only arises when there's conflict.

That's an excellent recipe for tension. It's a big part of why conversations about money are identified as a primary source of stress in a marriage. Many people are uncomfortable talking about money in the first place, even when times are good. And when times aren't so good? It's easy for "discussions" to devolve into arguments about needs versus wants, adjustments to current versus previous spending, savings, and general current spending versus future planned spending.

Emotions and behaviors play a crucial role—all of these are interrelated. Even the best financial plan will fail due to poor communication, and excellent communication isn't enough to offset bad financial fundamentals.

Learning to have effective money conversations *now* means you'll become equipped to work better together to navigate life's hurdles. And it doesn't matter whether you're in your early 20s and just starting on your own, or you're in your 40s, and you've been married before—**getting both partners on the same page is easier when the partnership is still new.**

You might start thinking a little more deeply about your relationship with money for the first time. Or you might need to figure out how to align your long-held values and beliefs with those of your partner. Maybe a major goal is mapping out a savings plan to buy your first house, or you're more mature and already have a lot of "stuff" that includes 401(k)s and other retirement investments.

Different partnerships have different factors that require different conversations, leading to different solutions and decisions. You'll build communication skills that will pay dividends in areas well beyond finances.

And you'll feel like you're truly in this together—because you are.

Who is this book for?

Anyone who makes financial decisions in a partnership can benefit from this book, whether you're in a traditional or nontraditional partnership: engaged, married, living together, or living apart. Also, this book isn't designed exclusively for people who have money troubles or debt-management problems. It's designed to help you *prevent* them, in addition to reaching your goals. But you'll likely get the most out of this book if you're in one of the following three groups:

- **Good, stable income.** Bills and living expenses are manageable—there aren't major debt issues, but not much is left for discretionary spending. Let's say 10%-20% of income every month. This group needs to make tough choices to build a financial future that meets their goals.

- **HENRY (High Earner, Not Rich Yet).** This group has a higher income level, with maybe 40% or more of income left over after necessary expenses. Still, they don't set aside much for a rainy day. The significant challenges for this group are creating SMART goals—specific, measurable, attainable, realistic, and time-sensitive. And identifying if they will do it. This group may want to buy a house, start a business, continue their education, upgrade their home, or even pay down principal on their student loans and other debt. To get there, they start aligning these goals with their core values to form a realistic plan.

- **Inconsistent income.** This group includes people in sales, business owners, and real-estate agents.—those whose income can vary significantly from month to month. Balancing expenses and income is a challenge, and planning is essential.

All three of these groups often find themselves kind of stuck in the middle: They aren't exactly one paycheck away from being destitute, but the future might look very different if they don't get serious about finances inside their partnership. They're not struggling, but they need help to create a realistic plan.

Typical financial books, programs, or websites that target these groups focus on investments while ignoring the other moving pieces of the puzzle. That's a bit like only maintaining the engine of your car, but never checking the tread on the tires, changing headlights, or even washing the thing. (OK, we maybe guilty of that last part.) Some of this "expert advice" consists of a constant barrage of tidbits of information. Still, it is never enough to put a real plan together and execute it. Or the "plan" is geared around selling you stuff. "Free" financial guidance isn't really free—we operate from the principle of no free lunch, as we'll talk about later.

By focusing on more than money and considering partnership TEAM resources, this guide can help you move into a fourth group: **The group that has it all together.** This group fully understands what they have now, where they want to go, and how they can get there.

What this book is—and isn't

The Most Valuable Wedding Gift provides a foundation for your partnership. As a starting point, it's a resource of information that will help you two understand each other's values, beliefs, have productive conversations about money, and make better decisions. Just as important is to recognize what this book *does not* have.

● **This book does not have all the answers.** It's designed to help your partnership develop a process with your partnership, including specifics regarding your situation.

● **This book does not have lectures about your bad decisions.** We assume you want to improve your conversations, decisions, and behaviors and not dwell on past mistakes. (And we know you're capable of making good decisions because you're reading this right now.)

● **This book does not have lectures about what's "right."** We aren't here to impose our morals, principals, and beliefs on you or dictate how to spend your money. We limit assumptions on how your partnership should operate.

● **This book does not contain personalized investment advice or recommendations.** Any investment is potentially good or bad, depending on your goals, risk tolerance, and other factors. Without knowing you personally, we can't provide personalized investment guidance.

● **This book does not have sales pitches.** We aren't going to try to sell you investments or insurance products or services. We want you to feel free to focus on your communication, plan, and, ultimately, your decisions.

Things to know before we get started

Before we move into the heart of *The Most Valuable Wedding Gift*, here are some key things to keep in mind.

- **You're not going to magically make more money because of this book.** Making money is about several factors, including open communication, developing your financial IQ, employment, spending and saving habits, wise investing, etc. This guide is about looking at the big picture first, developing a realistic plan for your future, and making better decisions.

- **We will operate under the assumption that you want to maintain your current lifestyle or better going forward (including retirement).** Drastic lifestyle downgrades are not easy—especially later in life.

- **This book is mainly about mid- and long-term goals.** Your partnership can potentially use some of these concepts to see results immediately. Oher concepts, however, you might not realize the full impact until years or even decades from now.

- **It's important you're comfortable with the concept of "it depends."** Today, the way we receive information feels black-and-white; in real life, though, there's still a lot of gray areas. *Both good conversations and better decisions require context and nuance. You will notice a lack of absolute statements (always, never, everyone, all, none, best....)*This program will help you understand the gray areas and find solutions that fit your personal circumstances.

- **Money is more than a measuring tool.** Money is a means to facilitate the other areas of our financial lives. Like the circulation system in our body, where blood carries nutrients to various areas, money does the same for the moving parts of our finances. Just as more blood in our system won't necessarily make us healthier, more money won't necessarily make our lives better. The goal here is to help make the *decisions* that allow you and your partner to live the life *you* want.

- **Since this book is designed for the two of you, we generally mean the partnership when we say "you,"**

- **This book assumes that both individuals treat the relationship as a *partnership*,** one in which each person's values and opinions are discussed and considered when important decisions are made. We assume honesty and transparency throughout the partnership.

- **Both partners are prepared to use their TEAM resources together.**

But please do not interpret this book as providing everything you will ever need to know to do it all on your own. While some of you can and will manage your financial futures, long-term planning in a partnership arrangement is complicated. These topics are typically emotionally charged, and there is a lot at stake. Be very, very cautious in trying to do this by yourself, and utilize licensed, credentialed professionals where appropriate.

The three basic principles

Finally, we ask that you follow three basic principles throughout the book—principles that will serve you well long after the last page. These are central to the Behavioral Financial Advice™ Program by think2Perform®.

1. **You are responsible for your decisions.** But not necessarily for the outcomes—you don't always have complete control over the results.

2. **Uncertainty is certain—there are no guarantees.** We don't know what will happen in the future, so your partnership should prepare for uncertainty.

3. **Your values should drive your decisions.** Let your shared personal values guide your financial decisions.

You might feel like everyone else has it all figured out—their goals, values, finances, etc. We are here to tell you that's not true. But even if that *were* true, you're on your way to getting there, also. So relax. We're glad you're here.

RejecTED Talk: Money Conversations

I received an invitation to a wedding from a friend. Who doesn't enjoy weddings? What I don't enjoy: finding that perfect wedding gift. Sure, you can use the wedding registry, but does a blender or beige queen bed sheets really capture the importance of this life event? We want to celebrate the wedding but also give them something they will need and will use.

So what is the most valuable wedding gift you could give couples? Realistically – help regarding *money conversations.*

So I search online for anything addressing money conversations, but the topic was too hot for Ignite and too taboo for TED. How taboo, you ask? People would rather discuss sex, politics, religion, and race relations. In fact, some people would rather talk about their own **death** than money conversations.

It's not just a 3rd rail topic—we are tied down, with half the fuse gone, and the train is coming!

We know the Statistics:

- Money is the #1 cause of stress in adults. [Northwestern Mutual (2020)]
- Money is the 3rd leading cause of divorce. [CDFA (2013)]
- 60% of families do not have a budget. [NFCC (2014)]

We all know this, but no one is **_talking_** about it. Who is going to give engaged couples and newlyweds a helping hand? Couples don't even have good sources to turn to for help.

I have to be honest; G**gle let me down. Advertisements and articles all focus on budgets and communication but nothing that addresses the other moving parts. Even Y*uT*be was a mess. Some crotchety guy, calling people names and insisting that I pay off my house today to become **debt-free**. Another told story after story about her success but never delivered on what we need to do to become successful or pull it all together. Some are great at motivation but don't offer much regarding an actual game plan.

What about our parents? The previous generation is in a tough position with regard to financial advice. Many were raised in a pension plan environment, so they don't have much experience in this age of stock options, multiple careers, self-funded healthcare, and 401(k)s. And even the parts they _do_ know, well, sometimes children aren't exactly ready to receive this advice from parents.

And what about financial advisors, you ask? The financial advisors I know, have an investment minimum. They offer investment advice but rarely address communication within the partnership, the couple's non-financial values system, social capital, and the behaviors that affect decisions outside of the couple's investments.

Who can help with marriage and money conversations & decisions?

CPAs, insurance agents, and bankers all know their specific area of expertise, but can they help couples with the big picture?

And **therapists and counselors**? We know they're great at addressing the psychology regarding relationships, but they rarely venture past budgets on the financial side.

If we have the technology to order pizza with G**gle glasses, we should be able to help couples out with finances inside their marriage, right?

I don't know.

But if I had *my* way, I would figure it out. I would give them a guide, just a couple hundred pages of what couples really need to know regarding cash flow, investing, communication, and joint decision-making from licensed, certified, experienced professionals but in layman's terms.

And absolutely no investment commercials, sales, or implied obligation. Just education. Built for newlyweds but applicable to engaged as well as seasoned partnerships. This dream guide would entertain, disclosure, and generally overview what we need to know regarding money conversations just like you were talking to your own family.

Yeah, that's what it would look like.

The Most Valuable Wedding Gift.

Communication

When it comes to marriage and money, it makes sense to start with the basics of communication. Communication provides the foundation for a strong partnership and collective decision-making. With two people, there are two ways of thinking, perceiving information, processing details, and making decisions. This doesn't change when it comes to money or how you feel about money. It's important to discuss your values, feelings, and relationship as they relate to money and finances. The way you feel about money will also mature, as your other thought processes, patterns, and mental maps mature. The initial step is to get on the same page. Then, you can grow together as you evolve individually, and just as importantly, collectively. The way you manage and view money will change, perhaps more than you realize, so let's start with both of you on the same page as it relates to money.

Checking-in

Let me ask you a question. Do you ask your partner how they are doing or tell them how you're doing daily? How does it make you and your partner feel when you have a regular check-in? Checking-in isn't a revolutionary idea, but regular check-ins are important, especially early in the relationship. **The first six months can really set the standard for how you two will communicate over the rest of your partnership.** Your partnership can and will evolve or dissolve based on how you two interact. At the end of this chapter, I encourage you to have a check-in conversation. It's easy just to let this pass by. Still, the habit of regularly asking each other how you're doing is valuable.

Here's why: You now have two decision-makers, whereas before you only had one (you). Think of yourselves like restaurant owners—perhaps one of you is a better "chef," more creative and inspired, while the other is a better "maître d'," able to plan and keep track of the big picture. You each contribute in your own way, but to make everything run smoothly, you also need to understand what's going on with the other person.

In the workplace, we see this as clear as day. How many team meetings have you been a part of when smart, capable people "bog down" due to failure to communicate? In a partnership, though, "team "meetings are frequently undervalued, at least in the beginning.

I know because I undervalued check-ins myself when I first got married. Communication? As a quant type, I thought: "that's fluff stuff" related to money.

Numbers are numbers, right? I did not realize how important it was to communicate effectively in a language my partner understood, and for them to communicate in a language that I understood. I'm not a therapist highlighting communication to keep the peace. This is a financial guy telling you that communication **absolutely** impacts your finances. It's important to give just as much attention to communicating and emotions as it is your finances. Communication impacts your decision making in both positive and negative ways.

Your Communication Skills

I can already hear people say, "Roderick, **I have** strong communication skills." Well, that may be true in some situations and not necessarily in others. When working with clients, I'm at my best because I'm learning about them, their needs, and their goals. That's at work. But at home, sometimes my "good communication" turns into too much focus on what *I* was saying, and my listening skills go to sleep.

Unfortunately, this can happen to anyone—and it's probably happened to all of us at one time or another. Just ask anyone married 20, 30, 40 years or more. **Good communication isn't a "set it and forget it" thing. It's an ongoing skill that you should consistently and consciously develop.**

Verbal and non-verbal communication

It's not just what you say – it's how you say it. Non-verbal communication matters.

When working with couples, financial professionals typically don't address money communication within the partnership. I've always found that odd because it's incredibly important. And that goes for both verbal and non-verbal communication.

When I mention money conversations – a segment of us turn the focus to investment terms and concepts. However, studies show just one word can have a dramatic impact on how we communicate beyond the actual word. *How* you say things -- visual, auditory, and kinetic cues, pitch, pace, volume, and emotion impact a significant portion of communication. Another component are non-verbal signals such as: eye contact, posture, gestures, and facial expression. [Mehrabian, A. (1981)]

Question: Has non-verbal communication effected your partnership communication this week? If so, what were the signals?

"Honey, let's make a budget."

A simple statement like this from one partner to another is typical in the early-stage of a partnership and money conversations. However, partners are often not aware of how a statement like this can be interpreted and trigger unexpected reactions in the other person. Reactions that often go beyond the actual words spoken. For example, a simple statement such as "Honey, let's make a budget" can lead to feelings and expressions such as the following:

- *"Great, you think I'm spending too much money."*
- *"I feel ashamed because I KNOW that I'm spending too much money."*
- *"I feel embarrassed because I have no idea how much money I'm spending."*
- *"I feel defensive because I shouldn't have to justify my spending if it's my money."*
- *"I should be making more money, so we don't even need to have this conversation."*
- It may even bring up feelings of fear, maybe: "*I haven't told my partner that I want to go back to school and/or start my own business. How do I do that now*?"

Any of those thoughts could roll around in someone's head just from one simple suggestion to make a budget. Those thoughts tie directly to some pretty deep feelings, and thanks to how our brain works, the other person may start to physically react before their thoughts even have a chance to form into a rational reply.

We're not asking you to ignore those feelings. We'll acknowledge them and move towards objective thinking and making sound decisions, respecting how we feel individually and collectively.

This is a partnership, and learning to make sound financial decisions together leads to making your partnership stronger.

Dealing with Emotions

You know that good communication—whether it's about the budget or something else—will benefit your short-term and long-term financial picture. So how do you get past the emotional response to keep conversations positive, or at the very least keep difficult conversations productive?

You can't eliminate or avoid the emotional response entirely, to be honest. But you can take steps to decrease the chance for it to derail the conversation.

1. Understand what your partner actually said.
2. Recognize what you're feeling at the time.
3. Understand how your feelings affects your response.

It's helpful to step back and ask yourself a few questions:

- *"Am I reading more into the statement or question than what my partner actually said?"*
- *"Do I truly understand the intent here?"*
- *"Is there something going on with me that is making me respond this way?"*

Maybe something happened at work. Maybe your past experiences make you fearful of what your partner is proposing. Maybe you have a low energy level. All those things can prevent a productive conversation from occurring. However, if you understand and address them, you can move forward.

For example, let's say your partner brings up a potential real estate investment. Your partner may not know that before your partnership, your family had a bad experience with real-estate, and you have been hesitant to make those kinds of investments ever since. Instead of letting your fear and emotions drive your response after hearing the "real estate" trigger. First, ask yourself the questions above—and relay to your partner what you feel and why you feel it.

You might say something like: "I've had bad experiences in real estate before, so my initial reaction was '*no way*.' It really scares me, but let's talk more about it. Why do you think it's good for us? Does it fit into the framework of our goals?"

Here's the good news: Your partner can help you recognize these emotions. In fact, they may recognize them before you do. The better you are with recognizing, reflecting, and reframing your words before you respond to each other, the higher likelihood for good conversations and making solid decisions, based on what you want and not your emotions. [think2Perform® (2018)]

Analytical vs. Emotional

In a perfect world, both sides of the partnership bring different talents to the table regarding marriage and money. Success reflects more than the ability to balance a checkbook. One partner may have some investment knowledge and understanding of the moving parts of finance. The other might have strong communication skills and emotional intelligence— things that are often undervalued. Given that people come from different backgrounds and walks of life, before becoming a union and collectively making decisions, you first want to understand yourself.

- Who are you, and what type of person are you? How do you process information? What do you value most in life?

What technical skill sets do you have that aid in financial decision-making?

Much of the information crafted for this book is designed for people in the middle—people who have a general background regarding money but are not necessarily experts.

For example, let's assume that both partners fall into two different segments. Let's say that *you're* the analytical type. You're the numbers person. You may work in a specialty finance field, like banking, real estate, insurance, or accounting. If someone had recommended a guide like this before my wedding, I would have responded, "Money conversations? Yeah, I talk about money for a living. I've got this. I work in this field; I know what I'm doing." But the reality was, I discounted the other aspects, such as how psychology ties into money or the emotional component. And when I use words like "emotion," "communication," and even "self-reflection," your natural reaction might lead you to think it's only the touchy-feely stuff that isn't important in marriage and money. Because numbers are numbers, right? But the opposite is true: Those **emotional, connective components are vital to money conversation because they will heavily influence your decisions**. The connection between marriage and money is an emotionally charged subject. If you don't connect on both levels– you will not carry the two.

Or maybe *you* are the emotional type. You tend to make decisions based on how you feel rather than a spreadsheet. You score high in emotional intelligence. If it feels right, it must BE right, because who can argue with gut feelings? People in this group might actually have a physical reaction to certain trigger words, so your partner should be cautious about how your emotions affect how you receive information. You bring your ability to communicate, your emotional awareness, your understanding of your values and your morals, and your principles to the table. The partnership needs your contribution, too.

Throughout my career, I've had the opportunity to witness couples from the perspective of a neutral third party, observing how the partnership interact. I embrace the fact that one of you may identify as more of the analytical type and the other more driven by emotions. I encourage you both to do the same for each other.

Questions:

- What is your personality type, and how does it help or hinder your money conversations?
- How can your love language or the way you recognize appreciation from your partner impact your communication?

Rules of the Road: Tough Conversations

As I've worked with marriage counseling & therapy communities over the last several years, they've provided some near-universal principles and effective communication strategies. Talking about money is tough; there's no doubt about it. But we'll close this section with a few communication "dos" and "don'ts" that can help—and they'll probably help in other areas of your life, too.

DO use 'I' statements versus 'You' statements. "When X happens, I feel Y." This makes your concern about YOU, not the other person. You own your feelings, and you are sharing them. Using "you" statements can feel accusatory and make it hard for people to engage. "You did this." Or "You didn't do that."

DO try to see the other person's perspective. Putting yourself in the shoes of the other person will go a long way toward reducing conflict. Then flip it, and ask your partner if they can try to understand from your perspective. Remember, you can see and understand another viewpoint WITHOUT agreeing. But if you continuously question without trying to understand, it can feel like distrust.

DO identify your money triggers. These are words that prompt uncomfortable feelings when it comes to your finances: budget, credit card, wealth, debt, bills, and other things like that. If you really want to dig a little deeper together, you can talk about the first instance of feeling these triggers and what caused them. This will help build even more trust and understanding.

The "cranks" are actions and behaviors; the "triggers" are words.

DO 'rank your cranks.' If you talk to any married couple, there are things each partner does that REALLY get underneath the other one's skin. Then there are things you don't like but aren't that big a deal. Identify what those behaviors or actions are for yourself and write them down. Keep it short and straightforward, maybe just the top three or four. Also, find out what the biggest cranks are for your partner. Maybe it's when they feel misunderstood, accused, or feel they aren't being listened to, heard, appreciated, valued, or consulted.

DO agree to disagree. I know that's a tough one for a lot of people. We all want our opinion to "win." But agreeing to disagree is a vital way to honestly and diplomatically identify values within your partnership. If the topic is important enough, you might want to seek a professional to help you through a disagreement or conflict. For example, mediators are used in all kinds of situations; they aren't just for divorce proceedings. No matter your communication styles, you can find a way to communicate that allows each person to feel heard and respected. A useful phrase to use in this situation is, "I may not agree, but I understand."

DO the active-listening exercise. Remember, listening is part of communication! The better you're able to actively hear what the other person is saying—and vice versa—the more effective your communication and partnership.

Active Listening Exercise

You're each going to give 60-seconds of active listening to your partner.

Notice, I didn't say talking exercise—emphasis on active listening.

Now it may sound simple, but you might find this takes a little more work and patience than you expect. Look at each other - really look at each other. As a side note: Experts say you should look at your loved one every day, for at least 30 seconds, without interruption to realize how much you need the other person and what they truly mean to you.

So look at each other, and I want one of you - the speaking partner, to talk to your listening partner about something that you're interested in.

Pick something comfortable that you can go on and on about for about a minute. Don't pick a contentious point in the relationship, just something you feel good about and comfortable spending some time chatting about.

Now, the person on the right: you are the Listener. I want you to listen. Nothing more. No verbal communication, but you can acknowledge what you hear with nonverbal cues. You can smile, nod, things like that.

OK? So again, 60-seconds starting with the partner on the left. You talk to your partner, and at the end of 60-seconds, the listening partner will review what the speaking partner talked about for 60 seconds. The idea is to gauge how well you were listening.

Ready? Go.

(After 60 seconds)

Alright. To the person who was listening - How was that? What did you hear?

Note – the exercise is not about what they were trying to say. How well did you do? How did you feel? Talk about it with your partner; otherwise, this was a passive reading exercise. And you on the left. How was that talking to someone who wasn't responding verbally? What did it feel like?

Now I want you to go through this exercise the opposite way, switching roles. The person who was listening is now the person who's giving 60 seconds on their topic. The person who was initially speaking is in active-listening mode. Again, do not respond with verbal communication.

Now, as you can see, this is a challenging exercise when you are not emotionally invested. You can only imagine how this exercise becomes a lot more difficult when you have emotions and feelings and backstories involved or when in conflict.

So as we can see, active listening is challenging and will take a little bit of work. However, once you've mastered the skill, you'll reap huge dividends, not only in your partnership, but in the workplace, and generally social situations you come across. People love active listeners.

What You Have: Cash Flow and Net Worth

To set the stage for money conversations and decisions within the partnership, we want to create a clear picture of **What You Have**. In order to simplify things, I'm going to incorporate imagery beyond the standard accounting terms and concepts you may expect to hear.

Let me paint a picture.

Let's say you open a restaurant in town. And it just so happens that a couple of years later, another owner opens their restaurant right next door. You even share a wall. The two establishments share some of the same customers, but you're both successful in the specific type of cuisine that you offer. You sell American cuisine, and the other restaurant sells Asian fusion, for example.

When your competitor first moved in, you were concerned because you thought, "The last thing I want is another restaurant right next door!" But you've come to find that people tend to speak well of both establishments. Over the last eight years, you two have had good times and bad times. And you've gotten to know the owner pretty well. You're on amicable terms.

In fact, it's not uncommon, after a long night, for you to share a drink and commiserate over the ups and downs of the local economy. The two of you are beginning to get even friendlier.

And, lo and behold, you both think, "What if we combined our two restaurants into one place?"

Eventually, your daydreaming evolves to a point where you actually start to move forward. But you also realize that a move like this, merging two established businesses, is complicated. So you bring in a specialist—typically a mergers-and-acquisitions specialist—to help you both with this transition.

In this case, we're going to walk through the various components of this special merger. And I'll tell you: it's more than great cooking, stellar service, and marketing. On one end of the spectrum, you have all the tangible things involved in your business—the building, the furnishings, the money, etc. And on the other end, you have the abstract things you experience as a business owner, such as joy, commitment, and a sense of pride in being a business owner.

But there's a lot to consider between those two extremes.

To help navigate this transition, you may require a little "leveling." That is, you may want to think about your vision for the partnership as you think about what your merger will accomplish.

There are two key pillars in the development of a plan for your new "restaurant." One is an assessment of what you actually have to work with *right now*. We'll call it your statement of financial position, or the partnership net worth statement, or your blended balance sheet. They all mean the same thing. The other document I like to look at is an analysis of where the money has been going, the joint cash flow statement. However, this is not a budget. I'll talk about the difference between these two later on.

Analyzing these two statements provides a lot of insight into what's going on with your current stand-alone businesses—what you have to work with—before you start to put together all the moving parts of the new business.

In the "*off-the-balance-sheet*" section, we will address the third aspect: items that both you have that impact your money conversations. Although you two are in the same neighborhood, even in the same building, there are clear differences in how you approach your business.

Blended Balance Sheet

Let's start with the balance sheet. Your blended balance sheet is like a piggy bank or a collection of piggy banks to fund your future goals.

To start the discussion about your balance sheet, I want to clarify the meaning of two key terms: "assets" and "liabilities."

An asset is property that is owned.

A liability is a recognized claim against or amount owed by a business or person. This refers to the legal responsibility to repay debt.

DISCLAIMER: Possession Does Not Equal Ownership

I want to make it clear that there is a distinction between something you "possess" and something you "own."

Just because you possess something doesn't mean you own it outright. There are items you "have" in your possession, like your house or car, but another person or entity has a claim against it. Those other people or entities are called lienholders. The amount of money you owe against the item in your possession is a liability.

Some people know these terms like the back of their hand, and others cringe when they hear some of these technical terms. So let's split the difference and use a map to help you understand these terms. If you can think of the numbers of your finances corresponding with areas of the map, you may visualize your partnership balance sheet differently than a dry, non-descript spreadsheet.

The Map Example: The Blended Balance Sheet

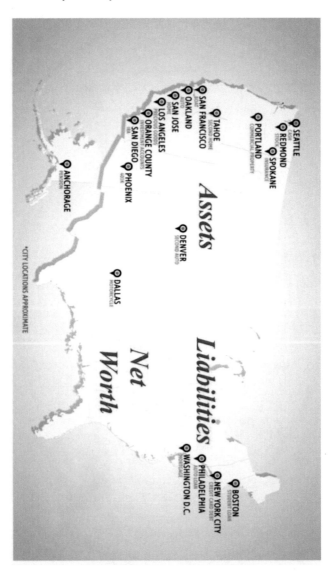

We're going to take this map and split the country down the middle. Assets represent the West, and liabilities and net worth represent the East Coast. My apologies to Cleveland!

Again, assets on the left, liabilities in the top right, and net worth on the bottom right. Assets minus liabilities leaves you with your net worth.

Assets – Liabilities = Net Worth

What goes on your blended balance sheet? It's important to understand where things go and how some components of this map will tie into the decisions you'll make later. Note that balance sheets are measured at the end of a period – typically at the end of the year. Some call it a snapshot of your finances, like a picture taken on a phone.

Common Assets

While your list of assets will vary, the most common assets for Americans include:

• Cash, checking, and savings accounts
• Stocks, bonds, and mutual funds (taxable accounts)
• Individual retirement accounts (IRAs)
• Company retirement accounts and pensions
• Insurance with a cash value
•   Real   estate/properties—primary   residences,   rentals, timeshares, secondary properties, etc.
• Physical items owned, such as cars, boats, jewelry, home items, etc. (personal assets)
• Privately held companies

All of these items can land on your partnership balance sheet. You can call it your balance sheet, or statement of financial position, or net worth statement. They all mean the same thing.

Where would you put your cash? The money in your wallet, in your car's ashtray, and under the seat cushions is cash. Then you have your checking and savings accounts. We're going to put all of those funds in Seattle.

You might have company stock. Since a particular company in Redmond, WA made a lot of people wealthy; we're going to put that in Redmond.

You may own some stocks or mutual funds that aren't in a retirement account but in a taxable account. That's just a regular brokerage account or investment account with any firm. Boom! Orange County.

So one type of tax-advantaged investment retirement account is called an "IRA." Let's put that in San Diego.

Do you have a 401(k) account or another type of company-sponsored retirement account? That goes to Phoenix, where perhaps you two attend baseball spring training.

Also, keep in mind that if you have a pension, it has value, even though you may not receive a physical statement. Put that in Anchorage, off the grid, but definitely valuable.

Now, if you have insurance with cash value or value apart from the death benefit, we're going to put that on the balance sheet over in Spokane.

For illustrative purposes, let's say you have a commercial property. We're going to put that in Portland.

You have other assets called "personal-use assets," and the No. 1 personal-use asset that most people have is their primary residence: their house. We're going to put that in San Jose.

Then you have your vehicle. Let drive across the Golden Gate Bridge and park it in Oakland.

Maybe you have a boat or another water vehicle. We'll dock that in San Francisco, in the marina.

Anything else? If you have another car, park it out in Walnut Creek. A vacation home? A second house? We'll locate that in Tahoe, for tax purposes. And then, if you have any kind of precious jewelry, art, or collectibles, store that in Los Angeles – on Rodeo Drive.

These are all of your personal assets. And to make everything simple, all these assets are in the Western half of the country.

Common Liabilities

Now let's move to the other side of the country. Just like assets, liabilities vary depending on your partnership, but common liabilities for partnerships include:

• Mortgage against their personal or commercial real estate properties
• Auto, boat, and other loans (or leases) for possessions
• Debt for unpaid medical bills
• Student loan debt
• Credit card debt/other unsecured personal debt

Let's identify your liabilities now, which we'll situate in the Northeast of the map.

To make this as simple as possible, we'll start with any credit card balance. We're not talking about the minimum payment due within 30 days; we'll include the balance that wasn't paid at the end of the period. We're going to put that over in New York City.

Have a student loan? Boston's a big college town, so let's put that liability in Boston.

Next, we'll locate any kind of auto loan or amount owed on a lease. Detroit would naturally fit here but to keep it on the coast - let's put them in Philadelphia – the city of brotherly love.

And then your mortgage, we'll put that in Washington, D.C.

Again, these are all items where money is owed versus the things that you possess. The house is the asset; the mortgage is the liability.

Net Worth

Any positive difference between your assets and your liabilities will give you your net worth. Some good times, let's say, in Florida. Maybe you enjoy the East Coast of Florida, by the ocean, like in Miami, Fort Lauderdale, or Palm Beach. Or you can also spend some time on the West Coast of the state, in Tampa, Clearwater, or St. Pete. Regardless, net worth is any difference between assets and liabilities. Note, net worth can be negative if liabilities are higher than assets.

Here are a couple of things to think about. Even though we just used a map, as an illustration, all of this is your nest egg (see the map's Southeast portion). Your nest egg is a substantial factor in how you're going to achieve your future goals as a partnership, such as a home purchase, retirement, or continuing education.

Your assets minus your liabilities equals your partnership net worth. Use this map as a reference.

Joint Cash Flow Statement

The second document that is essential to understanding **what you have** is the cash flow statement. Instead of a snapshot at the end of the period, cash flow is like a time-lapse video showing what happened to the money coming in and out of the partnership, from the beginning to the end of the measured timeframe.

For the cash flow statement, I don't have any fancy analogies or visual metaphors. Instead, I hope to give you clear examples and approachable language to help you understand cash flow. Cash flow is the basis for the ins and outs of your life's partnership.

Not the "B" Word

Notice our choice of words. Even the wording itself, "cash flow," is important. In fact, when I address money flow in and out of a household, I typically avoid the "B" word—which is "budget." I believe *budget* has a negative connotation because it's an expectation of what you **should** spend your money on. In my experience most people generally don't like to be told how to spend their money.

As an analyst for Smith Barney in the early 2000s, I would occasionally join financial advisors in their meetings with their high-net-worth clients. I remember a meeting with a couple in LA that was selling their business. The advisor was reviewing all the services his team could offer them. I'll never forget the conversation.

The advisor said, "By the way, among all the services we provide - we also help our clients with budgeting." Remember, I'm the analyst, so I was watching and processing everything. The husband kind of leaned back and an indignant look appeared on the wife's face as she waited for the advisor to finish.

And I remember her reaction like it was yesterday. She said to the advisor, "Honey, we're selling our business for eight-figures" with an independent tone. "We don't need you to tell us how to spend OUR money." It was eye-opening to watch this successful couple react to the word *"budget"*—they took it as someone telling them how to spend their money.

That's *not* what we're doing here. Again, we are merely laying out the landscape with cash flow to understand your money flow. We want to understand cash flow before we have any conversation about what to do in the future. Cash flow is a very good indication of the kinds of decisions you're making and may indicate your value system towards money.

We're going to use the phrase "gross income" for any money coming in. For some, it's the amount from an employer, called your W-2. However, income can also include other things, such as:

- Earnings from independent contract work -1099 labor (side-hustle)
- Rents from a rental property, or short-term rentals
- Passive income from securities, such as dividends from stocks and interest from bonds
- Royalties—possibly through earnings from entertainment.

Before we start to put expenses in categories and sub-categories, it's essential to understand three aspects:

1. Is this expense reoccurring or a one-time occurrence, like a wedding ring? You'd be surprised how many one-off

expenses families can have over the years—they are significant, but they are not usually repeated in the foreseeable future.

2. Is an expense consistent or variable? Your rent or mortgage is pretty much static every month versus the variability in an electricity bill which might fluctuate throughout the year.

3. What are your needs versus your wants? Or, in economic terms, we call this discretionary versus nondiscretionary spending. I think everybody can understand how distinguishing between these two is important, but the definition each individual uses within the partnership is not always clear.

Are you familiar with Abraham Maslow's hierarchy of psychological needs, like basic housing, food, and clothing? [Maslow, A. (1943)] Those things are nondiscretionary. Unlike some discretionary expenses or "wants" think about the ice cream at the end of your dinner. That's a decision you make purely for fun, but it's easy to miscategorize it as a "needed" food expense.

Life isn't a binary proposition: black-and-white, all-or-nothing. For example, where does a haircut fall on the spectrum? Is that discretionary or nondiscretionary spending? What about a car payment? Or new clothing? These are areas for discussion. These ideas play into our value system and illustrate why it's important to connect values with goals and decisions.

One note, if a service or a good is thoroughly used in a period – it's generally considered an expense. If the item is used in future periods, we may consider it capital. Capital may appear on the balance sheet (car, house, jewelry). This is where depreciation comes into play.

The ability to account for your outs is critical for any analysis. Classification is dependent on how you use the information, but generally, expenses can fall into these main categories: home, personal, insurance, entertainment, auto, taxes, and outside interests.

Finally, we'll define an expense as any product or service that is completely used in the period. If a product is used in future periods, we may categorize it as capital and represent it on the balance sheet.

Debt

Since we're talking about where your money goes, let me address the elephant in the room—debt. A majority of the conversations around marriage and money—from the money gurus, Y**T*be channels, or random articles you run across—have to do with the use of credit and the management of debt. Let me give you the big picture of what transpires when you use credit cards to cover your purchases.

Not all plastic is dangerous. When you use your debit card, the payment comes directly out of your bank account. But in the credit-card category, there's a cost to it, and that cost is in the interest rate. From a fundamental standpoint, debt is like any other tool or resource. Whether you're talking about debt or electricity or a motorcycle, whether it's good or bad depends on how you use it.

If you are the average age of people getting married today, you've already been in the workplace for a while. You've established your credit history and your habits in using credit cards. And frankly, you've also formed value judgments about credit cards. I don't work for a credit card company, so I'm not going to spend a lot of time explaining what credit cards do and using them. But credit cards or revolving lines of credit have advantages and disadvantages, depending on what you do with unsecured debt.

Advantages:

1. Accounting/Tracking. Want to better understand your cash flow? Pull info from your credit card statement and compare it with your checking/saving accounts.
2. Ease of use: Don't like carrying around cash and change? Plastic can help.
3. Perks: Miles/rewards.

Disadvantages:

1. Credit cards are easy to use, making impulse buying REALLY easy. (We'll address behavior in another section.)
2. If you don't pay off the balance, interest charges apply.
3. Credit cards may make it easy to lose sight of how much you're spending—putting down $100 in cash feels different than simply pulling out your card.

Whether credit cards are good or bad hinges on whether you pay off the balance within the payment cycle, if you do, you don't pay interest, and you probably collect points for using the card—so you've effectively beaten the system. If you don't pay off your balance in full every month, you haven't necessarily lost, but now you've incurred a cost. The outstanding balance becomes a liability on your balance sheet and a hole in your proverbial piggy bank. And, the interest will increase your total liability over time.

In general, credit card use becomes an issue if:

you incur debt – meaning purchases that are not paid off in the current period — AND there isn't a corresponding asset AND no formal plan to reduce it in the future. The interest on the debt is like a running taxi meter.

But sometimes credit card debt can make sense. Let's say you're going to buy Seattle Kraken hockey season tickets in April, which are $10,000 for two seats. If you simply pay the $10,000 in cash, you'll have no finance charges.

If you pay for the tickets with credit with an annual rate of 10%, you'll incur about $500 in interest over the next six months. Now, in six months, if you can sell those tickets for $10,500 or more, you offset the finance charge with the profit. However, if only sell them for $8,000, you incur a loss. *

See the difference? Paying by credit is effectively keeping the cash and creating a liability with a running clock with the borrowed money.

*assuming ticket scalping laws are observed.

Sample Joint Cash Flow

INFLOWS

Salary—Partner 1	$_____
Salary—Partner 2	$_____
YE Bonus —Partner 1	$_____
YE Bonus – Partner 2	$_____
Total inflows	$_____

OUTFLOWS

FICA, federal and state income tax	$_____
401(k) plan contribution	$_____
IRA traditional contribution—	$_____
Apartment rental payment – (Or Mortgage)	$_____
Electric	$_____
Phone, internet, wireless	$_____
Health Club	$_____
Household Goods	$_____
Health insurance	$_____
Renters insurance (Or Mortgage Insurance)	$_____
Auto loan	$_____
Auto lease	$_____
Auto expense/maintenance	$_____
Auto insurance	$_____
Disability insurance	$_____
Credit card payments	$_____
Student loan	$_____
Food	$_____
Entertainment	$_____
Vacation	$_____
Clothing	$_____
Gifts (Birthdays & Holidays)	$_____
Total outflows	$_____
Net cash flow	$$_____

For Illustrative Purposes Only

Partnership Balance Sheet Liabilities & Net Worth Example

		Assets		
		Current Assets		
		Cash	$x,000	
p¹		Checking	$x,000	
p²		Checking	$x,000	
JP		Checking	$x,000	
JP		Savings	$xx,000	
				$xx,000
		Investable Assets		
p¹		IRA	$xx,000	
p²		401k	$xx,000	
p¹		Insurance	$xx,000	
p²		Company Stock	$xx,000	
				$xxx,000
		Personal Use Assets		
JP		Home	$xxx,000	
p¹		Car	$xx,000	
p²		Motorcycle	$x,000	
JP		RV	$xx,000	
JP		Jewelry	$xx,000	
				$xxx,000
		Total Assets		$xxx,000

Partnership Balance Sheet Liabilities & Net Worth Example

	Liabilities		
	Current Liabilities		
P[1]	Credit Card (X.xx%)	$xx,000	
P[2]	Credit Card (X.xx%)	$xx,000	
			$xx,000
	Long Term Liabilities		
JP	Mortgage (X%)	$xxx,000	
JP	Line of Credit (X.xx%)	$xx,000	
P[1]	Auto Loan (X.x%)	$xx,000	
P[1]	Student Loan (X.x%)	$xx,000	
			$xxx,000
	Total Liabilities		$xxx,000
	Net Worth		$xxx,000
	Total Liabilities &Net worth		$xxx,000

P[1]	Partner 1
P[2]	Partner 2
JP	Joint Partnership

Budgeting in LA

In 2001, I was promoted from regional investment analyst to divisional investment analyst, with the opportunity to move up an income tax bracket. This promotion also required me to move from my hometown of Seattle to Los Angeles. Cultural differences and professional advancement aside, I wondered how the move to L.A. would impact my overall finances. I anticipated more ins (income) but potentially and probably more outs (expenses) as well. At the time, websites gave some inflation adjustment numbers, but that didn't really help tell the whole picture. I needed more details.

Luckily for me, my former manager, Jim, who was working for a different firm, grew up in L.A., and he had a better understanding of my situation. He gave me this advice:

Jim: "*Look, Roderick, it's really simple. Cultural norms in L.A. are a little different than Seattle. So let's say housing* (I owned in Seattle but would rent in L.A.). *Right now, you're spending about 20% of your income on housing. In L.A., you should expect a minimum of 35% but probably closer to 40% of your gross income to go toward housing.*"

He saw my eyes widen.

Jim: "*Hey, look, where you live matters.*"

I conceded, "*I guess there's some value to that.*"

Jim: "*Second, I know what you drive (a 14-year old Honda Civic). Well, in L.A., you are what you drive, and it completely matters. So that's another 30% to upgrade your car*."

My eyes got even bigger.

Jim: "*And then speaking of your clothes, yeah…*" Now in the investment industry - suit and tie are required. At that time, let's just say I was in the middle to lower tier of the suit and tie game.

He continued, "*Look, you're going to be brought into meetings with people at a high level*."

Ultimately, I was meeting with people worth high seven, eight, & even nine figures. "*Even though you're an analyst and manager, you'll need to step up your professional wardrobe and more or less your social wardrobe. You have to move on from that Nirvana look*." (For the record, I was a big jeans T-shirt and Steve Madden shoe guy, and I was beginning to wonder if he appreciated my world-class charm.)

"*And if I had to spitball - at least 25% in the first year and a 15% allocation each year after that .*"

I never claimed to be a math whiz, but at that point, I had to stop him.

I said, "*Wait, 35% for housing, 30% for transportation, and 25% for clothing? What about everything else? Food, entertainment, heck even emergency funds and savings?*"

His reply was coldly matter-of-fact. "*Oh yeah, all that will be 35% too.*"

Six-Figure Income & Millionaires

Wash Your Hands

Let me pause and emphasize an important point. If you look at your partnership financial picture - cash flow and net worth (aka balance sheet) in the short run, you may not notice a glaring issue. You two are managing your debt and increasing your net worth — the overall health of the economy until the current pandemic — your job, stock market, and housing marketing are still stable.

Your challenge is in the intermediate and long term. You are not on pace to maintain your retirement lifestyle — for 20-25 years - despite your high income. Remember, income variability is a challenge over your work-life.

Some of you understand the importance and urgency. Some of you are just realizing the issue. And some will simply respond, "*yeah, but that's in the future — we'll figure it out*. For the last group, let me help you with that with a PSA.

Let's say you find out — someone you think you know reasonable well — doesn't wash their hands — and when they do — it's about 10-20% of the time. Now there's a segment of you — who'll respond — Annnd?" and I'll reply with my value statement, "that's gross."

For everyone else - you are as shocked and disgusted. So you ask them, "Why don't you wash your hands?" And they respond, "why? I'm not sick, I'm doing just fine."

In the short run, you may not feel the effects. But in the long run – everyone is better off.

Partnership planning is about; Understanding what you have, where you're going, and how you are going to get there. And if you are not on track – even with a high income – you'll want to prepare for the future, or other words, **Wash Your Hands**.

Six-Figure Income and Millionaire

We've addressed tracking where your money goes. Now let's talk a little about your cash flow—more specifically, **how much** money is coming in? Because cash flow includes both the ins and outs, right?

There's a standard set in our country that *six-figure income* or *income above $100,000* per year is a badge that says a person has "arrived." Today, it's less rare for a household to bring in *six-figures* compared to forty years ago. In Seattle, the median household—excluding households headed by a single adult—earned $121,000 and $161,000 with children in 2017. [Balk, G. (2018)]

Recognizing the importance of these benchmarks, I'd like to provide perspective on the six-figure income benchmark and the holy grail "*millionaire.*"

As far as the term "millionaire" goes, this number is significant, but not well defined.

- Is a millionaire a person(s) that makes a million dollars, or is worth a million dollars?
- Is that based on total assets or net worth?
- Does the net worth include the equity in their personal residence or private business?
- Does it refer to a million dollars of liquid assets?

A house, a business, or a portfolio of marketable securities may have the same "value" but have different characteristics like liquidity and marketability. And the horseman of inflation will steadily chip away at that million over time as we will cover in the Do-What-You-Want Section.

Here's why I bring this up: Most people would consider a household with an income level over $100,000 and on pace for one million dollars at retirement as golden. But we often forget the other side of that equation: what are they spending and what are their liabilities? That's the part that isn't clear to outside parties, and sometimes even to the involved parties.

Financial planners typically request clients' monthly net cash flow as part of their analysis. It may surprise you how many people don't know that number - for a variety of reasons. Possibly because both parties aren't disclosing all their expenses, or maybe they haven't tracked expenses together at all. It's not so much the income level that defines success; the net number after expenses determines their financial plan's viability. Hence, just focusing on the gross income number for retirement has the potential to mislead regarding overall health.

Average income

Throughout this book, we reference "average" household incomes, which will vary depending on the region. This can range from $45,000 to $150,000 and above. For households in the $45,000-$75,000 per year range, it's easy to assume this book doesn't apply. "We only make……" is a typical response. I understand but let me provide an additional perspective. Do you plan to increase your income in the future? Some concepts in this book may have a greater impact as your partnership income level increases, but they *do matter at your current income.*

But have you ever thought about the number 75,000? That isn't small on an absolute basis. Try counting to 75,000. What about 30,000? How about 10,000? You may see $1,0000,000 far removed from $75,000 annual household income level. However, that's roughly the amount you will have earned without any pay increases from the time a child starts kindergarten until they graduate high school.

Boat Mechanic

This book does not explicitly instruct you how to make more money, and it certainly covers concepts that are not money-related. Some concepts are complicated. Some people have asked me to write a more focused, less complicated book. Some have even suggested I'm doing people a disservice by not making another personal finance book for those who are not "in the six figures" so I'll use this analogy.

Let's say I'm an engineer that works on boat engines. My skill set fits a particular sized boat that has specific needs. Since I don't live on the water, I drive ten miles to work every day. I make an average living for my family and donate time and money beyond my work. But every week, I pass 3-5 cars on the side of the road, having car trouble. Once in a blue moon, I'll stop to help a stalled car, but on average, I drive by, even though I probably have the skill set to fix their problems. It might seem obvious to some people, but we can't serve everyone to their specific needs.

There are plenty of books that delve into the specifics of budgeting, credit scores, debt management for individuals. However, this book is designed to have a less technical feel **with** higher-level concepts to bridge the gap between psychology and finance. Bridging this gap can benefit those who need more than debt and budget help, including middle-class partnerships.

Titling: Who Owns What

When it comes to what you bring into the partnership individually, some partners focus on when mine and yours becomes "what WE have." You may ask, "Why are we talking about who owns what? It's all part of the marriage, right? And we're planning for *forever after*, so it's not necessary." Remember the principal: planning for the certainty of uncertainty. These concepts regularly arise in the financial planning industry. **This book does not offer legal advice; these are simply observations and questions to ask** each other and engage a professional when appropriate.

Many partnerships approach marriage with the idea that everything is joint property, split 50/50, down the middle, as soon as they say, "I do." Is that really the case? It's an attitude that works well on a practical level within the relationship, but two institutions, banks, and courts play by their own rules. Have you ever noticed how bank or brokerage statements identify different accounts? There are clear indications of who "owns" the account or how the asset is titled.

That's why it's such a hassle if someone isn't listed on the account. It matters. And, of course, if you two decide in the future to put the wall back up and revert to two "restaurants" – the courts have their rules and procedures that guide how assets and liabilities are divided. Marriage laws are specific to each state, so what you hear from friends and family or even online may not apply in your situation. Even titling effects taxes through how income is treated. Consult your legal and tax professionals to understand who owns what.

If assets are not titled correctly – and someone passes away – do you assume all the remaining assets go to the surviving spouse? You would be surprised by the stories that come out of the act of probate.

What are some ways you can protect your partnership?

- Name the appropriate party (which could be each other) as beneficiaries on bank and investment accounts.
- Develop a will.
- Leave instructions on what should happen to your assets once you die.
- Draft a **power of attorney** for financial decisions for when one of you is not able to make sound choices.
- Draft a **power of attorney** for healthcare decisions when someone isn't able to make sound decisions regarding their health. Health directives are designed, so they are only valid or in force when deemed necessary by a medical professional.

What happens to assets when one or both of you are no longer living? Titling will determine where your net assets (assets after liabilities are paid) will go and who will receive them. The point of naming beneficiaries and wills is to avoid probate. Probate is the process of sorting out who gets the money. If beneficiaries aren't named – such as family/friends or charity – the money goes to the federal government. **The old saying in estate planning - If you don't make estate plans, someone else will make plans for you, and you probably won't like it**.

Your partnership money will go to one of three places when you pass away: to loved ones, charity, or the government. How does it currently look?

If you don't know, your advisor/CPA/or estate planning attorney should be able to help. They can also help shape it the way you would like it to look.

Prenups

When it comes to what you have individually, your genuine concern is how and when it becomes "what *we* have." Sometimes, that means planning for a prenuptial agreement or prenup.

If two people are willing to sit down and talk about prenups, that's a positive thing. It shows they can have candid conversations about finances. The word prenup can be a trigger for people. If someone refuses to talk about finances before the marriage, you may want to think about the potential financial impact of your union, based on the state in which you marry and the state in which you plan to reside.

One common concern about addressing the topic of marriage and money, including the dreaded prenup, is that it will upset the apple cart, possibly preventing the marriage. I've never heard of it happening, but a serious financial discussion may uncover future challenges when it does. For some, avoiding frank financial disclosure is akin to avoiding medical testing and disclosure. But avoiding conversations regarding marriage and money will not change the situation or the facts. Uncovering these challenges early on and identifying helpful resources is likely a positive move versus delaying the inevitable and setting yourself up for significant problems in the future.

The Evolution of Wealth

One of the values of this program is the ascension of expectations, both on an individual level and as it applies to the partnership. When a person graduates from their formal education, their first goal is to **find employment** or **get a job**. That sounds basic, but the best plans are useless if there isn't any money coming in. In this gig economy, I don't think we should discount employment - it is a goal.

Second, **how much money do you make**? Now, we're not supposed to ask others that question, but we should notice that income is valued in different forms. Some people tie their income to their self-esteem and their worthiness. We can measure income in several ways. How much do you make an hour? What is your annual salary? How much do you earn per project in this new economy?

The third is **total compensation**. Some firms find different ways to compensate employees. This could include deferred compensation at different levels, whether it's individual company stock, stock options, health care benefits, or other significant benefits. This compensation could represent an opportunity for significant ownership in a company. Benefits can include perks like travel, meal expenses, a company car, and paid vacations. The benefits of entrepreneurship are valued differently depending on the group.

The next one is a big one. **It's not how much you make - It's how much you keep**. When you start moving up tax brackets, the value of a partnership reveals the difference between individual and married status. Tax professionals can help you recognize these differences. Some people make a significant amount of money, but they also spend a significant amount of money. There isn't always a clear transition from thinking about making money ("the bag" or income) to creating wealth (net worth) for the future. That's one of the values of this book, to helping people understand that relationship.

At some point, the income component starts to level out. The next question might move to how you hold your wealth. Is it held in real estate, or other hard assets, ownership of a company, financial assets in a retirement, or financial assets in a non-retirement account? Some might argue the value of political power could play a factor. Your ability to create and grow wealth continues and increase your earnings level through skillset and intellectual capital.

Then, as you start to move forward, there is an evolution in your financial profile and goals. You start to ask question: **What am I doing with this money?** Can we create enough wealth to generate enough passive income to live our lifestyle throughout retirement? That is the concept of retirement or Do-What-You-Want.

Because at a certain point, you can cover your own needs and provide for your happiness, and then you begin to evaluate: **How do I add value to others outside of my partnership and immediate family? Finally, what is my legacy?** What is my impact on the world after I'm no longer?

That is a difficult transition for an individual, but it's even more complicated to talk about finances for a couple. How do **we** start to make that transition? How can **we** remain mindful of our impact and what adjustments will happen? It's not a linear path. Things happen. Jobs change. Investments change. Different sophistication levels change for people, so they have different levels of attainment and different goals. We want to recognize this process of evolution when it comes to the pathway of your partnership.

OFF THE BALANCE SHEET

In this section of What You Have, we will identify items that aren't found on the Balance sheet or Cash Flow statement that impact money conversations. While many in the financial community focus almost entirely on financial goals, and ultimately products and services, in this section, we recognize these important "off-the-balance-sheet" items and concepts. They include values and beliefs, human and social capital, even Social Security and Medicare.

Social Security and Medicare

First, let's assume you (and your employer) contribute to Social Security and healthcare premiums out of your paycheck. Public-sector employers may offer different benefits, and those who are self-employed are responsible for both the employer and employee portion.

Will Social Security be around in 20 or 30 years? There are generally two camps: Yes, and it's implied that it will cover a significant portion of retirement expenses. Or no, because the system is broken.

No matter your stance, it's important to support your beliefs with research, verify the facts, and be open to reconsidering. In my professional opinion, Social Security's viability over the next generation will depend on some small—at the individual level—adjustments to the program. Adjustments to eligibility age, payment amounts, caps on income, or net worth. Medicare is similar: Changes are needed to restore sustainability, but the system is far from unsalvageable. Both are important for funding the "Do What You Want" period, otherwise known as retirement. We'll explore DWYW factors later in the book.

Many younger couples don't even think about these two things, because they seem so far away. But they need to be considered for planning purposes, even far into the future. In my financial planning practice through 2018, if I needed to ballpark Social Security benefits, I would assume enough to cover roughly 20% of total expenses for clients more than 10 years in the future. There are studies and analyses that give a more accurate assessment by various financial service firms.

Mind/Body/Spirit

While money is a significant component of this book, the reality is that the life components of Mind, Body, and Spirit are **interrelated** throughout this program. In this game called life, we try to coordinate all the moving parts. When experienced people offer guidance to those at the beginning of their careers, one of their biggest challenges is conveying the importance of interconnection. For example, a company's monetary compensation reflects what you give regarding your **ability** (hard and soft skills) and your **time**. There are hidden costs embedded in many jobs because of the nature of the work related to your health.

Consider this: *What are you doing for yourself?* The most significant investment you have is in yourself, or the two of you. What does that include?

While we are not dictating or committing to a particular set of values, the partnership's well-being encapsulates the mind/body/spirit concept. The spiritual aspect can shape money conversations and decisions in many partnerships.

In the realm of the mind, there's formal education, of course, but we also learn from our experiences as we mature into adult human beings. The mind uses these to help us grow us people and contribute to society.

With the physical body, there is a distinct investment of TEAM resources to consider. Generally, overall good health is important for the partnership. This includes the coordination and collaboration of a variety of elements: nutrition, your activities throughout the day (including while at work), sleep, etc. Your daily health-focused activities could be things like Pilates, yoga, free weights, kickboxing, running, meditation, or other exercise options. All have one thing in common: they require an investment of your TEAM resources. There is no free lunch.

What About Stress?

Stress is the pressure we experience that can impact our functioning—it results from a lack of resources to address differing intensities, frequencies, and durations of life demands. [DADS (2018)]

However, not all stress is bad. Positive stress is moderate and short-lived, causing brief increases in heart rate or mild changes in stress hormone levels. Learning to adjust to this type of stress is an important and necessary aspect of healthy development that occurs in the context of stable and supportive relationships. [NIMH (2018)]

"Tolerable stress" is severe enough to disrupt the brain architecture if left unchecked, but is buffered by supportive relationships that facilitate adaptive coping and mitigate the damaging effects. Examples include a death in the family or natural disaster. [NIMH (2018)]

Tolerable stress generally occurs within a time-limited period, giving the brain an opportunity to recover from potentially damaging effects. [DADS (2018)]

Toxic stress response can occur when a person experiences strong, frequent, and/or prolonged adversity—that includes *accumulated burdens of family economic hardship*—without adequate support. [NIMH (2018)]

Relationships can mitigate the toxicity of stress. [DADS (2018)]

Questions:

- What are some of the tradeoffs with your current job?
- What TEAM resources can you provide to advance yourself?
- Do you feel the elements of your life are currently balanced?
- If not, which areas are over- or under-allocating TEAM resources for the return you're receiving? How can you address it?

Values

If we are going to talk about finances in a way that doesn't involve a balance sheet, there is one crucial aspect that shouldn't be ignored: the different values you and your partner may have. We define values as principals, morals, and beliefs regarding money and the other TEAM resources within the partnership. As a reminder, this book is not designed to dictate what your values or beliefs *should* be. Instead, we are trying to identify what values are held by each partner and how each is prioritized. Not society values or ideal values, but your true personal values.

If I had to identify one thing in this book that is undervalued but *invaluable* for partnerships, especially at the beginning, it is identifying and aligning values.

More specifically, commonly held and prioritized values are nice, but recognizing your partner's values and building the ability to work through joint decisions is a primary driver of productive money conversations.

Here's an example of a value statement: "I believe in giving all of my immediate family gifts during the holiday season."

If one person strongly agrees with this statement and the other person strongly disagrees, we have a conflict, a source of tension. In my experience, if beliefs are shared, or at least one person is neutral, the misalignment of beliefs is less likely to lead to significant conflict. This applies to conflicts related to money or monetary values.

Some may view values as binary: either you have specific values, or you don't.

Instead of muttering, "I guess that how you were raised," another possibility is to try to understand the real impact of the belief, and to move the belief from the complete control bucket to the little-or- no-control bucket. Of course, depending on the seriousness of the situation, seeking professional guidance from a family counselor or therapist is an option.

The goal is for you two to have productive conversations, despite possibly holding different beliefs. Hopefully, the importance of aligning values in a marriage isn't foreign to you. If it is, let's start to work on that here.

Our values can shift and evolve. For example, when we were single or dating, we may have placed a high value on taking a road trip with our family or friends. Now, spending time at home, working on projects around the house, and other activities might be more important.

How do values impact your partnership? If an activity causes undesirable emotions in one partner, is that effectively communicated to the other partner? What emotions are they experiencing, and why?

An advanced analysis may show that conflict in the partnership isn't actually about the current difference in values over an event or an item. <u>One person may value the same thing differently over time.</u> For example, one partner loves peanut butter and jelly sandwiches. On a scale of 1 to 100, they give it a score of 95 today, a score of 75 in one week and 65 in a month, and 60 in any period after that. The other partner may also value PB&J at a score of 95 currently but 60 in a week and 30 in a month. One person may value things differently in the current period versus in future periods. Substitute PB&J with retirement assets or buying a house by a certain age, and you can quickly see how these differences in values can pose a problem.

Whether your passion is cars, cooking, horses, or gardening, it's important to recognize what kind of value you place on it and the TEAM resources you commit to it inside your partnership.

Values Exercise

One of the most important exercises in a new partnership is identifying and aligning values. Understanding each person's history with money, morals, and principals helps to guide partnership decisions. And alignment is not just recognizing what common values are prioritized, it's also finding a way to incorporate them productively into your decisions.

Exercise: Write down your values (principals, morals, and beliefs) separately and compare them.

Advanced Exercise: As you two identify goals, values, and beliefs, is there a time constraint that causes the value to rise or fall in priority? If you two feel you need to assign a number for your Do-What-You-Want chapter in your life, what is the value of obtaining these goals at a specific date/age?

- How do you work through different beliefs, mainly related to money, between the two of you?
- Regarding vacations: What do you like to do to escape from work? Lay on the beach, explore a new location, Jet Ski, or a combination of several activities?
- What are your views on borrowing/lending money from family/friends?
- What is your policy for friends/family staying at your home?
- Do you feel obligated to send cards/gifts for graduations/weddings, births, and funerals?

Something to think about:

Many people may assume that your environment or where you grew up explains the origin of your values. However, other variables factor in, like age, gender, and friends ("birds of a feather flock together"). Preferences shaped by social media and other sources beyond immediate family may play a role as well.

How do these variables shape your values? Write for 10 minutes and then compare answers with your partner.

Human Capital

Depending on your current job and your career goals, you two can start estimating how much you hope to earn given your particular set of skills. But we often don't consider the "human capital" in our lives. This refers to the value of our skills—both hard and soft—in the open marketplace.

Your ability to earn is usually based on your set of skills and your overall ability. However, technology and needs in the workplace are evolving to the point where many workers need to switch careers or start a side hustle if they are willing to update their skills. This aspect can impact your future family finances. Some people learn a particular set of skills early in their career and mold their career path around those skills, regardless of the relevancy. We will address this later when we talk about adult continuing education in the "Goals" chapter.

Partnership Income – Does Our Income Move in a Straight Line?

One of the challenges to planning for future goals is the volatility or inconsistency of income streams in the future. Some might point out partnership employment prospects and earnings potential is not as consistent as previous generations.

For most people, the ability to fund future goals outside of the short-term and intermediate time frame is dependent on your partnership's earnings potential. We all have our mental accounting of what we can afford regarding house payments, retirement, and even starting a family, based on our best guess about what our earning potential looks like. To put it simply: employment prospects are typically not constant.

Employment is primarily dependent on three factors outside of direct experience:

1) Education level—degrees and certifications you've earned.
2) The industry or sector—some skillsets have a higher value and greater opportunities in the open market than others.
3) Age. For example, if you work in marketing as a website designer, a 25-year-old may be viewed differently than a

65-year-old. However, when giving investment advice in wealth management, the reverse can be true. Running for a state senate seat at age 30 may be considered too young, while a 30-year-old football running back may not command the same contract as a younger running back because age 30 is labeled "over the hill" in the football community.

Generally speaking, employment prospects = education + industry +/- age

Of course, specific hard skills and individual social intelligence will heavily factor into employment prospects. Have you two discussed your current and potential future value in the open employment market, given where you are today? More specifically, how are you two addressing your continuing education?

A word of caution on your career: Career progression and life balance go together. You may want to think of your career in chunks in addition to your entire period of employment. Circumstances change, and our challenge is to work on the things we *can* control. Let's remember the people formerly employed at companies that no longer exist who thought they were going to ride the wave of technology for the rest of their professional careers, and ended up looking for a new career—sometimes late in their lives.

Understanding Your Value/Human Capital

Do you know someone who is integral to their organization, but is uncomfortable when it comes to asking for a raise? They are undervaluing their human capital. Another co-worker may earn more because they are better negotiators—even though they are less valuable to the company.

On the other side of the coin, you might need to have a challenging conversation with your partner if they are *overvaluing* their own skillset. For example, if your partner believes they are the best salesperson in the world, but they haven't made a sale in months while their co-workers are making sales left and right, it might be time to discuss accurately describing their performance and what they need to do to improve. It goes back to the allocation of TEAM resources. It's not an easy discussion to have, and it might threaten their ego, but it can help manage expectations regarding the future. This ties into overconfidence, which we readdress in the chapter about behaviors.

The beauty of human capital is that it doesn't remain static. Technology allows us to learn and improve with less restriction on location and time. If you or your partner are serious about learning new skills, you can consider online education options. You might also choose to listen to podcasts and audiobooks about the subject or sector, as well. It might take some time and energy, but that investment could pay off exponentially.

Your Personal Human Resource Department

Some partnerships place an expectation on the other partner to contribute TEAM resources to the partnership in specific ways. This is especially true when it comes to household income and rearing children. The art is to balance the ability and the time, energy, and money to feed into your happiness quotient. Think about your partner as your co-personal human resources account. How do you tap into that? How do you support each other in your respective careers? When/how does one partner compromise personal objectives related to the partnership? And while some career paths are not linear, does one matter more than the other? Based on what criteria? Do you have a realistic assumption of your earnings potential going forward?

These are tough but important discussions to have with your partner.

Social Capital

There's a good chance that you've heard the term "social capital" before, and it's an integral connection with your personal & partnership decision making. The "capital" here doesn't refer to actual finances—it refers to your standing in your community around you. Social capital broadly includes the aspects of effectively functioning social groups, such as interpersonal relationships, a shared sense of identity, a shared understanding, shared norms, shared values, trust, cooperation, and reciprocity. Social capital is often highly dependent on social intelligence. [Goldman (2014)]

Emotional intelligence, maturity, and competence are important and are directly manifest in our efforts to maintain or create social capital. For example, let's say that one partner insists that both of you attend several birthday functions, potlucks, and other social gatherings because they value their tribe/group/friends. What are the TEAM resources allocated to these events? Do you need to bring a gift/dish of food? What about travel to and from the event, and the time spent at the event? What is the benefit? The answer may lie in social capital. Aside from those in sales, who may view attending as an opportunity to network, most people will not expect a direct economic benefit from attending a social function. But there are multiple reasons besides the chance to see friends, catch up outside of social media, or just enjoy social interactions.

Do you agree with this statement? Why?

Do you consider attending or "making an appearance" a deposit into the bank of social capital?

Conversely, what effect does *avoiding* events have on your partnership? If your partner never attends the social events you care about, it might begin to feel like your values aren't aligned. Also, if you compromise to the point where you don't socialize nearly as much as you did before your marriage, it can affect all sorts of personal and professional relationships to the point where it affects your social capital as well.

Social capital doesn't just have to be about events—maybe it's sending the right Christmas and birthday gifts at the right time. Social capital applies to many situations throughout your daily life. We sprinkle our day with activities that, at the very least, serve to maintain our social capital. We join friends/co-workers for dinner. We send thank you/sympathy cards; we attend weddings. Social capital isn't the *only* reason we do these things, but there is an element of personal/partnership gain. Therefore, when we spend TEAM resources, the benefit goes beyond having a meal, having some fun. There is a higher benefit. This pandemic has revealed the value of community and social interaction beyond the food and drinks we consume.

Ideally, your marriage will increase social capital for *both* of you. Still, there are situations where you or your spouse simply don't have the time or energy to maintain your social standing with all of your friends, colleagues, and acquaintances. You'll want to identify and discuss what events to attend and what to forgo.

Examples of Social Capital

An example you might have seen or experienced in your personal life, or through popular culture: One partner becomes so obsessed with their marriage that they end up becoming demanding and unreasonable. This often leads to them straining their relationships.

Some partners can attest to the fact that their significant other was "challenging" at one point in time, and they may have even spoken to them about it at the time. However, a partner that genuinely understands social capital knows that this day has the potential to be the most important in their life and respects that.

Even though their future lifelong partner might be described as "slightly less than agreeable," the less than emotionally involved partner may have the emotional intelligence to understand, "This isn't as important to me, but it's important to them." This kind of empathy is essential to a successful partnership.

Another important aspect of the conversation is to recognize that marriage is not only important to people because it's a "special day"—it's an important milestone for social capital, as well. A marriage is a celebration of having found a partner for the rest of your life, and there's a sense of pride and community involvement. For some individuals and couples, the wedding may represent a new stage of stability and maturity that they have achieved.

The question that often guides these decisions is who will help you in a time of need. Another related question: *What TEAM contributions have you or your partnership made in your family, friends, faith-based organizations, community, or other groups?* In times of need, who can you count on? If you are sick, who will visit or bring items to you in the hospital? During financial trouble, who can lead you to resources? Need a wedding gift that addresses one of the biggest obstacles in a partnership? We'll address the challenge regarding the taboo regarding the topic of money later in the book.

Typically, social capital matters to everyone, to some extent—but it's up to you and your partner to have the difficult discussions about what obligations take precedence, and what compromises you are each willing to make.

You don't need to make a spreadsheet every time a social obligation comes up, but you might find that a little discussion can go a long way. Sometimes, it might only take a few minutes to realize how and why a particular event is significant to your partner's life, and it can help you to reframe your perspective.

Let's be honest here: there are situations where you disagree with your partner on which events are "important." One partner might insist the other attend their work party, or the other partner might get upset that their partner isn't spending more time with the in-laws. Either way, a successful marriage means that two people are able to align their values. Here are questions to ask yourself:

Questions:

- How close are we to the people involved?
- Are we obligated specifically to attend this event (are the two of you honored guests somehow, for example)?
- How much do we both want to go, and is there a disconnect between our interest levels?
- Can you two compromise?
- How important is this to my partner, and why?

Goals: Real Estate

Goals are dreams with "wheels and a roadmap"

Before you move on to the investment vehicles and retirement section, take time to reflect on your intermediate and long term goals. Consider using the traditional, tried, and true **SMART** goal formula:

Specific: What, when, and why.
Measurable: This is where your performance metrics come in to help you know when you accomplish your goal.
Attainable: The requirements necessary to achieve your goal.
Realistic: Acknowledge the roadblocks that would prevent you from reaching your goal.
Time-sensitive: Start and (most importantly) end dates.

Take some time to reflect on your core values related to your goals. What's more important: goals or processes? Maybe you are asking the wrong question—the answer is both. Goals and process go hand in hand. It's difficult to achieve one without the other. Have a starting and endpoint for your goal, and a way to measure what you want to achieve. Also, you may have different timeframes. For example, you can have short- and long-term goals. It's up to you to define each timeframe. For example, "short-term" might be three, six, or 12 months; "long-term" think five or ten years or even longer.

Real Estate

Both real estate and college education represent a blend of goals, values, and investments to people. People use real estate for many reasons, many of which have nothing to do with the monetary *value*. For example, people buy homes to experience the "home" component, such as raising a family, entertaining friends and family, and making memories. Others buy homes strictly for investment purposes.

Later we will incorporate the two when evaluating a potential mortgage and paying back student debt.

As a reminder, our mission isn't to give you the "right" answer regarding these two areas as a standardized test. This guide is designed to help your partnership explore the discussion points, including questions to consider as you move toward better conversations and making better decisions.

Looking at the "Why" behind Real Estate

The real estate market in areas across the country can be downright unaffordable. However, whether you're looking to buy, sell, manage an investment property, or simply transform your existing house into the home you've always wanted, there's one question you should ask yourself first. (Hint: It's not about square footage, market trends, location, or even your budget.) Above all, ask yourself:

"Why?"

This topic is generally reserved for real estate agents or mortgage bankers. But for years, I've incorporated real estate into clients' overall financial picture to model its financial impact. Realistic financial plans are not dependent on investment asset levels.

Besides, I've had multiple real estate agents, a couple of general contractors, and an architect as clients, so I've gained insights about their business. Toss in a financial background and the incorporation of economic data, we can now approach real estate from different perspective. The key here is understanding the partnership "why" question regarding real estate.

In most cases, the answer isn't as straightforward as you might think.

"We don't like the kitchen, bedroom, or bathroom in our other place."
"We want an entertainment area or a backyard for our dog."
"The neighborhood schools are the primary factor that drives our decision."
"My parents made a lot of money in real estate"

One primary reason that isn't always articulated is the most fundamental need for "shelter," which falls into the "safety" category on Maslow's hierarchy of needs outlined earlier.

Some people want to purchase a property simply because homeownership is a status symbol, declaring to the world, "We made it."

Another reason for purchasing property is for the investment. You may value the expected returns on real estate higher than other asset classes, making it a "buy" option. You may also feel your hard-earned dollars could be maximized in different places, making it a "sell" option.

Therefore, the question is:

"How does primary personal real estate fit with your other investment vehicles to help you reach your goals from an investment perspective?"

If that question sounds like skepticism, you may want to revisit the behavior section regarding bias.

Many people ask, "Isn't real estate one of the best investments you can make?" with a prejudgment built into the question. Earlier, we identified how our history (or beliefs) with money drives our goals and, ultimately, our decisions. Some people view real estate as a guaranteed return on investment. Like any investment decision, it's important to consider and confirm variables as you move forward.

One technique I picked up early in my career is to ask people who are knowledgeable in an area but do not have a financial incentive for their input. Before buying a house, do you talk to neighbors regarding the house, the neighborhood, the schools, or the public services? How many do you ask: one person or five different households?

Speak with an Appraiser

Related to real estate, you may want to speak with a real estate appraiser. Note that some websites provide home price estimates based on the average price per square foot in that city, and others base them on the average price per square foot for the zip code. Both are estimates and do not account for the home's unique characteristics. While this may seem like a small nuance, the farther you are from the average, the more room there is for error and possibly inefficiency—both good and bad.

Real Estate = Good Return?

The same methodology for deciding the return of investment applies to real estate. Looking back on the last ten years of price movement is simply that: looking back. Return = purchase price + TEAM resources – ending price. As you two account for real estate through your cash flow and balance sheet, remember to account for your home at market value and the mortgage at a historical value minus principal payments made. Walkthrough your scenario with a professional to account for these various factors to help with your conversations and decision-making.

The Hassle Side

Regardless of your list price or the agreed selling price, buyers borrowing from a traditional lending institution have to justify the price to secure their loan. The bank doesn't want to lend on a property that a neutral third party does not agree is worth the risk. This can lead—and has led—to failed real estate transactions because the house didn't appraise for the agreed-upon sales price. Although the buyer agreed to the sales price, the lending institution would not lend that amount due to the final appraisal value.

Also, people have sold homes that have appreciated nicely, only to find they can't buy back into the same market. That's the hassle side of the equation.

On the other hand, you can move out of your primary home and either sell it or convert it to a long or short term rental, creating an income source for your joint cash flow. Remember that in most cases, managing a rental property has its own unique set of challenges and also requires TEAM resources.

If you decide to sell your *primary* home, then you may have the opportunity to exclude the gain from capital gains taxes. However, if you decide to move out of your primary home and convert it to a rental, the property may have a different tax basis and exclusion. Uncle Sam is the family member that plans to make a visit.

Net Worth

From an investment perspective, real estate is a potential hidden gem. Some households have significant personal wealth associated with their primary residence. The idea of leverage through a home mortgage allows partnerships to buy more (house) assets.

Along with the opportunity, you should consider the liquidity risk or the ability to convert a portion of an asset to cash (liquidity) and the ability to sell in a tough market (marketability). You should consider all these related to real estate purchase and selling decisions.

Retirement

Remember, real estate is an investment vehicle, a tool. There isn't an absolute right or wrong about it. However, what counts is how you apply and understand it in context to your risk tolerance and overall financial situation. When you buy real estate as your primary home and simultaneously view it as an investment prospective, there is a potential to become house rich (asset) and cash poor (lack of income) by the time you retire. This may force you to sell and move out of the area or implement a reverse mortgage.

Before investing, you may want to consider how real estate relates to your family dynamics (think children and multigenerational housing). Here are a few things to keep in mind when looking at a property's expected appreciation:

- Have a clear understanding of the *why*.
- How quickly will I need access to funds from real estate?
- Understand the tax ramifications.
- Where will you live after you sell?
- How does it relate to your family dynamics?
- How does it relate to your long-term goals?

Capitalization Rate (CAP) and Effort

Because real estate is in an entirely different asset class, the most important thing to remember about real estate is to compare apples to apples.

You might own a house, which you might have purchased as an investment. However, you can't calculate the rate of return on that investment without addressing what's called the *capitalization rate (CAP)*. Some people might stop and ask, "Do we really need to calculate a cap rate?" The answer is: absolutely not—if you don't care about a realistic return. (Note, technically the cap or capitalization rate is highly dependent on income received during the period and thus the formula is not as useful for partnership's primary residence where no rental income is received)

Quick math might lead you to think, "We bought our house for $300,000, and now it's worth $600,000, so that's a 100% return." First of all, unless you paid in full for your house, your cost is more than $300,000 due to the interest on your mortgage alone. Secondly, you also incur other costs and expenses related to home maintenance, upkeep, and improvements over the course of owning your home. The cap rate takes into account all of that, providing you with a more accurate picture.

Your goal for buying a home or property may be to have a place to live and sell it for specific amount above your originally purchase price.   That is a clear, specific, and measurable goal. However, it may not be realistic based on the timeframe. This greatly depends on how much you purchase the property for, the location, and the projected market value for the length of time you own the home. (Again, this goes back to considering your short- and long-term goals.)

Homes also require maintenance and upkeep in terms of TEAM resources: time, labor (Energy), ability (Expertise), and materials (money). Note, from a pure investment timeframe, it's also essential to account for the amount of time and effort the home or property will require for as long as you own it.

For example, let's assume you two buy a home for $300,000. It has three bedrooms, one and a half bathrooms, one-car garage, and located on a quarter of an acre of land. The home was originally built in 1950, but all the significant items are functional (the roof, the heating and AC system, the appliances, insulation, etc.). Other than a few coats of paint, some light renovations, and maybe a new kitchen floor, the property is relatively in good shape and is built on a solid foundation. However, you will want to address some of these important items over the next decade.

Next, let's assume that you will likely have to put in approximately $2,000–$5,000 per year into the home in terms of materials and labor costs to make improvements and updates over the next ten years. Include those costs over that timeframe, depending on things working and your sensitivity level regarding the previously mentioned items.

What about your time and effort, or the cost of paying for expertise? Mowing and edging the lawn might not take much expertise, but the effort may lead to paying the neighbor's kid or outsourcing the job to a professional. Do you know how to snake a drain? Paint a room? Build a deck? Your ability is part of that equation.

Let's say you calculate your total time worth a dollar amount for the next five years. Now, add your other TEAM resources to your purchase price. Now you're closer to the total value in terms of the purchase price and added costs you've put into the property.

Now, let's say you put the home on the market. Will the sales price cover your TEAM costs, plus the purchase price? Ultimately, this would depend on market conditions and the value of your home. Again, if your goal is to live in the home and sell it for 20% more than what you put into it (considering time, energy, ability, and the cost of material and labor), then you have a good idea of the return you can expect from the sale price.

Question: What about debt-free living?

Some partnerships view debt as an unwanted burden, so their goal is to pay off their home mortgage. Let's walk through the potential impact on the partnership financial picture. What percentage of your income does your mortgage principal and interest comprise?

Typically, mortgage principal and interest are **less than** 30% of your gross income. My experience: some people overestimate the actual cost savings of mortgage-free living.

Remember, insurance and taxes don't go away when you pay off your house. And utilities like water, electric, sewer, and garbage are a recurring expense along with maintenance. Also, paying off a house in 15 to 20 years without improvements means your house looks and functions 15 to 20 years older than when you first purchased it.

On the other hand, there are positive tax ramifications concerning mortgage interest and property taxes. Also, debt-free living likely has a positive psychological impact beyond the numbers.

If you want to purchase a home to start a family, make memories, build sentiment, and make updates along the way, then these numbers may or may not make a difference to you. In this scenario, you will likely focus less on the monetary investment and impact on cash flow and more on the *value* system, such as considering sentimental value, emotional connection, and embracing the "home" component.

Advanced: Commercial Real Estate

Let's say your partnership would like to purchase a piece of commercial real estate. The bank representative tells you what they will lend for this endeavor, but you two will want a good grasp on your financials. These financials include both personal and business cash flow statements and balance sheets, including the following components:

- Checking
- Savings
- Business plan with a marketing plan component
- Pro forma, or future income statement projections
- Primary residence
- Legal documents
- Business interests, including a business evaluation

You both are probably aware of your current cash flow, but projecting out business cash flow into the future can be challenging. You'll need to coordinate legal, tax, insurance, banking, and other aspects with specialists. One note: retirement funds are generally not considered as collateral for a business or commercial building loan.

Short-Term Rentals

Short term rental income accounts for income for more partnerships in the last decade. What are the variables that factor into the decision to rent a section or entire property? Take a look at a few more questions you should consider.

- What if your cash flow is better than expected? Should you pay down the loan?
- What are the costs to furnish, advertise, and clean the unit?
- What are the TEAM costs to respond to inquiries?
- What if the occupancy rate is 25% lower than projected?
- Should you lower the rent?
- What are the effects of insurance or general wear and tear?
- Does the additional cash flow outweigh the TEAM cost?

It's also beneficial to have someone looking ahead and "around the corner" on your behalf, asking questions that consider the *total* picture. Like other important decisions, communicate, run the numbers, and ask for expert advice if needed.

Looking at the Big Picture

Real estate has multiple factors related to the question *why*. This quickly becomes a game of Marco Polo. Remember the game, usually played in the pool and one person closes their eyes and shouts, Marco and the other kids in the pool have to report back "Polo" as the person who has their eyes closes tries to locate the other players. Sometimes the person who is it - is moving in the direction that is not closing the gap between them and the other players. Based on their direction, they are off. However, by shifting the angle or direction slightly, they can put themselves back on course. Related to moving closer to a solution - sometimes the question asked is not very helpful moving towards the solution. Instead of invalidating questions/search/or data sometimes, it's helpful to respond to your "Marco" with this "Polo" to indicate you may want to change your focus slightly to move more quickly towards a better answer or decision.

Another derivation is the saying "looking through the wrong end of a telescope," which I occasionally hear from Colin Cowherd, a sports radio/podcast personality. Which means you are looking/focusing on the little things when you really should focus on the big picture.

Goal: Continuing Education

Similar to real estate, the cost of college or higher education has also rising rapidly. Based on previous conversations, some individuals and families value college education as much as homeownership!

Of course, investing in education is important. However, when considering the college investment, it may go deeper than, "I'm going to go to college to get a good job and make a lot of money," or, "I want to send my son/daughter to college so he/she will get a good job someday."

In this section, we explore what you may consider regarding the value of a college degree and the value of the education you receive. This section applies to those who are considering returning to school, advancing their education, or even saving for their current (or future) children's education.

Enter a Field of Study

Why do people go to college in the first place? The typical goal is to receive a degree from a school or institution to enter a particular field. Plus, they expect a performance measurement associated with grades.

However, earning a college degree may not equate to the golden ticket of a good, high-paying position, or stable long-term career. Most jobs aren't static over an extended period; they grow, change, and evolve.

The truth is that each company and employer has their own criteria for assessing and interviewing candidates for a particular role. Generally speaking, managers want to add valuable employee assets to their teams. And here's a lesser-known perspective; Many managers do not enjoy sorting through résumés and dread the interview process.

Therefore, a college degree can be used as a proxy to address many hiring questions. Generally speaking -it is assumed that to earn a college degree, you will have competencies in a particular discipline and the qualities of being dependable, flexible, capable, and task-oriented based on grades and other accolades.

Is he/she competent, able, and versatile? Will he/she follow through on tasks? The point here is that a college degree might help get you in the door, but how far it takes you is up to you.

Your Network

One component of the value of your college experience is your **network**. When you graduate, the people that you met in college are valuable. In my experience, a large portion of hires come from referrals rather than random resumes. So, when checking off the boxes on the "find a job" checklist, knowing someone on the inside or who can speak favorably on your behalf is half the battle.

Here's a litmus test. Ask ten of your close friends or family about their current employment. Specifically, ask if someone inside the organization helped them to secure their current job. Then ask how many people received a job without knowing anyone at their current employer. The old phrase, "It's not *what* you know; it's *who* you know" is two-sided. Or network equals net worth. Both matter. Why is this important?

Your professional village matters. Developing and cultivating a network takes time and effort. You want to *add* value to your network; otherwise, you are just asking others for favors. Networking isn't exactly something they teach in a classroom. Various clubs, fraternities, sororities, and former student associations are prime examples of places where you can learn to network. Developing a flexible mindset allows you to embrace new learning opportunities, and people can bolster your value in the workplace.

Emotional Intelligence and Social Intelligence

Today companies are looking for more than a hard worker and fast learner. They also place a considerable focus on emotional intelligence or competence as an asset. Emotional intelligence and social intelligence are all about how you interact with others, even if they aren't in your formal network. It shows that you can add value as part of a team and that you play nicely with others. It also relates to how others around you feel or interact with you.

Worth it?

So, is college worth it?

A friend told me they were considering going back to school for a particular advanced degree after spending time in the workforce for more than a decade. We all have diverse beliefs about degrees and education. So I asked, "What TEAM resources are you committing to this degree?" It was a night program for three years *if* they were able to go straight through.

Next, I asked about the monetary cost of the program: $70,000 before loans. Student debt belongs to the partnership balance sheet, but it also factors into joint cash flow if financed.

What about the expected earnings potential increase? $10,000 a year in the next 3-5 years.

Finally, I asked what the value of having a Master's degree without regard to the increased compensation or access to different positions? In other words, what is the value of saying, "I have a Master's degree," or a law degree, or an MBA? What impact do you anticipate that you will have on your social network? How is your institution viewed in relation to other institutions? How much does that factor into your decision?

On the other hand, when considering the cost of college today, you may want to think about the benefits beyond the next 1-3 years. When preparing for, attending, and earning an undergraduate degree—or even continuing and earning a Master's degree or doctorate—you are talking about 17 to 19 years of total education. Once you factor in that amount of time, plus what your employer provides, is that enough to cover 40 years of potential employment years?

What skills are transferable in the job field? Are you able to keep up regarding technology requirements? Have you considered a vocational class or certification? What is your learning style?

Retirement: Catching Up with the 'Rents

Off-screen voice: Have you talked to your mother since she retired last month?

Roderick: *Oh no. I need to give her a call.*

(Roderick picks up the phone.)

Roderick: *Hey, Mom- how's it going?*

Roderick: *Good. Good. Hey, I was calling to say congrats on your retirement! Sorry, I wasn't able to make it to your retirement party – work has been crazy.*

Roderick: *But I want to make it up to you. I was thinking of taking you and Dad out for dinner to celebrate.*

Roderick: *No, no kids. Just you, me, and Pops. And I'm calling to find a day this coming week that works, now that you have all this free time. Monday is a bad day for me, so what other day works for you? Is Tuesday evening good?*

Roderick: *Oh, you have your Board meeting at your Community Club. Okay, how about Wednesday?*

Roderick: *Oh, that's your night for tutoring teenagers at the church. Of course. Well, what's Thursday looking like?*

Roderick: *Right, you have Pilates at Union Pilates.*

Roderick: *Oh, you want me to join your class? ....Uh Um I can't* *seem to find my workout mat. ..Can I get back to you on that one?*

Roderick: *Yes, I promise to think about it. So can we do dinner Friday?*

Roderick: *Friday night book club, huh? What are you reading?*

Roderick: *"The Salt-and-Pepper Murders"? I see. That's tempting, but I don't know......can you guys can fit me in over the coming weekend?*

Roderick: *Uh-huh, golf on Saturday and walk around Seward Park on Sunday. Quality time. That's cool. I totally get it. So what about the next couple weeks?*

Roderick: *Oh, you have the trips to Palm Springs and Tampa, Florida. I remember.*

Roderick: *And a week in Vancouver. I'd forgotten about that. Okay, when does your schedule open up?*

Roderick: *April?*

Roderick: *Yes, after tax season is over. Of course.*

Roderick: *Oh, okay. You sure stay active for a retiree! But I'll put us down for late April.*

Roderick: *Sure, I'll accept your calendar evite.*

Roderick: *One more thing? Sure, shoot.*

Roderick: *Of course you two can take the kids to the zoo on Sunday. Just text me when you decide on a time.*

(Roderick hangs up and shakes his head.)

Roderick: *(Speaking to himself.) So that's retirement. Huh.*

Do-What-You-Want
Four Horsemen

"You're likely to spend as much time in retirement as you did in all of your formal education – even if you've earned a law degree"

If you are in your 20s or even your 30s, you may not be concerned with "retirement" - it's a 20th-century term.

What are we really talking about? Doing What-You-Want (DWYW) The period formerly known as retirement. Chillaxing. Is that better?

But here's the thing, preparing for this period is a little more involved than paying off your house, more than contributing a couple hundred bucks a month into your 401(k). Remember: as a partnership, you two are responsible for this period of your life. We make decisions in the short, intermediate, and long term. This chapter is about the long term.

Myth
"If I can't control it - why bother?"
"I didn't plan, so I'll just keep working."
"I won't live long in retirement, so why bother?"
"If we have $1 million, we should be ok."
"I don't know all the factors, where do I start?"
"Social Security and Medicare should cover most of it, right?"

We'll address these questions –say it with me – "in order to have better conversations to make better decisions."

One area essential to almost any financial plan is the concept of retirement. We outlined how our needs and support as working adults have changed since the last generation in the "Choose the Right Advisor" segment, but now we can visualize what the "new retirement" looks like.

First, if you still have a vision of sitting in a rocking chair for 15 years, it's probably time to update your thinking. On the other hand, if you plan to die at your desk – we have an alternative to consider. A reminder, your goals should be SMART—specific, measurable, attainable, realistic, and time-sensitive—and define them within your partnership.

Retirement: The Box

To visualize retirement, I like to use a box to describe the variables to consider. Most of us want to factor in how LONG this box is— which means how long we will live. It might sound a bit morbid, and it's not possible to know precisely, but it's important to estimate our calculations.

This box is really a collection of different periods – let's define them as years. Within each year, your life is a little different. You'll want to use reasonable assumptions about future cash flow — what's coming in and going out. Your income sources likely will be more varied as time passes.

Of course, it's not that simple. There are four major challenges to this retirement equation, and four less major but still identifiable barriers— "little ponies"— to address. Become more familiar with each factor as you have your discussions within your partnership and product specialist. "Horsemen" and "little ponies" will help guide which product or investment vehicles to use to reach your partnership goals. After 22+ years of studying, teaching, and participating in the journey to retirement – I've determined that one shoe doesn't fit all, and we may need a collection of multiple kicks for our journey. The goal is to understand the challenges before you start evaluating possible solutions.

Longevity: Managing The Expectation of Your Ability to Work

The beginning of our retirement box—or the end of employment—requires you to manage your expectations about how long you'll want to (or able to) work. *"I'll just have to work longer*" is a typical response to retirement funding challenges, but as I'll show you, it's not that simple.

This comes from JP Morgan Asset Management *Guide to Retirement 2020*:

The statistics mentioned in this section are from the Employment Benefit Research Institute.

75% of current workers expect to retire at 65 or older. But the reality is that only 23% of workers actually do work until they're 65. [GTR 2020]

There's a technical term for that – uh oh.

To be fair, not everyone turns in their access card because they're essentially forced to stop, but factors like health problems or disability, changes at their company, or other work-related reasons certainly lead the pack. Some leave to care for a spouse. Then, a few hang it up because they just don't have marketable skills anymore.

Question: What age do you two plan to retire?

Life-Expectancy Probabilities

What about your potential longevity for the Do-What-You-Want period? For example, if you're 65 today, what are the chances you'll live to 75? Before I start, I can imagine some of you are ready to skip this because you think age 75 is OOOOOLLLLLD. I don't agree - but I understand.

So let me give you some perspective: If you are in your mid-30s, remember how you thought about your current age when you were 22. If you are around 30? Think back to what you thought of being age 30 when you were between your sophomore and junior high school years. And if you are younger than 30? First, I want to thank you for taking this seriously but if age 75 is a stretch, think of what you thought about your current age when you were 10. The point is, you will get there, and your perspective will change.

Back to the longevity horseman that challenges your retirement. Retirement is a challenge due to the uncertainty and unanticipated length of how long we'll be around. No one likes to think of death, but it's essential for money conversations beyond budgets.

The longer you live, the more resources you'll need to support those extra years of life. Today, it's not uncommon for people to need a full 30 or more years of income after retirement. In other words, it's typically best to plan for longevity.

This chart is from J.P Morgan Asset Management's 2020 The Guide to Retirement.

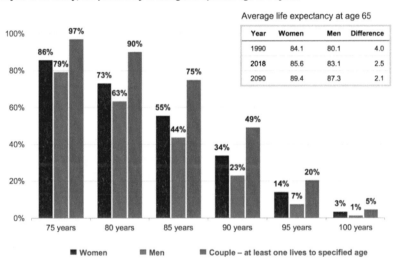

If you're 65 today, the probability of living to a specific age or beyond

Average life expectancy at age 65

Year	Women	Men	Difference
1990	84.1	80.1	4.0
2018	85.6	83.1	2.5
2090	89.4	87.3	2.1

Chart: Social Security Administration, Period Life Table, 2016 (published in 2019), J.P. Morgan Asset Management.
Table: Social Security Administration 2019 OASDI Trustees Report.
Probability at least one member of a same-sex female couple lives to age 90 is 56% and a same sex-sex male couple is 41%

Let's look at some numbers from the Social Security Administration. For those who are 65 years old TODAY, we can show the probability of lifespan for each gender and as a surviving spouse. Let's look at life expectancy benchmarks at 75, 80, 85, 90, even 100 years old. Along the bottom is how old you may live, and along the side is the percentage of people who are 65 today who will achieve that. This does not account for all the factors that determine our longevity, but it helps for illustrative purposes.

The purple bars represent females, and the grey bars represent males. The I'm-not-sure-what-the-dog-ate color bars represent the likelihood that at least one of the two people that make up the partnership will live to the specified age or beyond.

Back to our example, let's assume you're age 65 today. What are the chances you'll live to age 75 or beyond? If you're female, there's an 86% likelihood that you'll live to 75 or beyond. If you're a male, the likelihood is slightly lower: 79%.

Even if one of you passes on before age 75, the statistics say the surviving spouse or partner has a 97% chance of living to 75 or beyond.

Let's go to age 85 years. If you are female and age 65 today, there's a 55% chance of living to 85 or beyond, 43% of males.

Now, some of you guys might look at this and think, "I'm a male, and I have less than a 50% chance of making it to age 85 or beyond. Not great odds." Well, no, but if you're (better or worse) half of the couple in that household, then there's a 74% chance that someone will live to 85 years or beyond.

So just take that in. Statistically, it could be either of you. If you're female, just remember you have a pretty good chance of living to 85 or beyond. Also, factor in that there's a ¾ chance that someone in the household will live to 85 or beyond.

We use 65 as a retirement age because I know some of you are looking at that as the goal. But you should know that according to the Social Security Administration, the age for full retirement is not 65 anymore for those born after the 1960s, its higher. And the rules are subject to change in the future.

Starting at age 65 and living to age 85 or beyond will extend your Do-What-You-Want period for about 20 years or more. And when we're planning for the average couple, we want to factor that in.

To put it in perspective, think about how many years it took to get your education. If you have graduated from high school, that's 12+ years of school. If you add an undergraduate degree, you get credit for four more years - even if some finished a little faster or some of us enjoyed the college experience. Then, for those who get a Master's or other advanced degrees, add two more years, which makes 18 years of education. For a JD –law degree – that's 19 years. So 20 years of retirement is at least as long as all of that education. That's a long, long time.

Obviously, longevity factors into the significance of health care, coupled with inflation, and how extravagantly or simply we want to live our lives.

As you go further–say, to age 90—you see that 34% of women aged 65 will live to age 90 or beyond. That's one out of three women. Pretty good odds. 22% of men aged 65 today will live to 90, between 1 out of 4 or 5. I think the other interesting statistic that comes out of the age 90 section is that there's a 50/50 chance that someone in the household is going to live to 90. Just a coin flip, essentially, whether someone in your household who is 65 today will live 25 years or more. Not 20 years, but 25 years. That's some serious longevity.

A coin flip is acceptable for determining who gets the ball first in a football game or paying for coffee. But when planning for your Do-What-You-Want period, you might not want to leave it to that. If there's truly a 50% chance—a coin-flip chance—that someone will live 25 more years after retiring, it's important to do some really serious planning.

I applaud Katherine Roy and her team at JP Morgan Asset Management for putting this work together regarding the Do-What-You-Want period in the *Guide to Retirement*, presenting it from an individual perspective, and also presenting it as a two-person household.

The other thing: is the probability of one member of a same-sex household living to 90 or beyond. For females, it's 56%; for males, it's 40%. [G.T.R. (2020)]

So again, let's put that in perspective: 25 years. If you're considering retiring at 65—even if you're off by a year or two—statistically, there's about a 50/50 chance that someone will live to 90 or beyond. I want to emphasize that. And you need to pay attention to the possibility of "or beyond," not just the actual number. It's estimated that there are roughly 80,000 centenarians in the US. For realistic conversations and decisions, you may want to consider these statistics and other factors for more realistic plans. [GTR 2020]

TAXES

> **We want to be very clear; this is not intended in any way as tax advice. We are merely highlighting tax-related concepts that could impact partnership money conversations. Regarding your specific situation, you should seek personalized assistance and advice from a professionally licensed enrolled agent (EA) or certified public accountant (CPA).**

Since I already dived headfirst into the taboo area of marriage, money, and death, it won't hurt to address taxes. You may want to think about taxes as a necessary cost. I'll make a distinction between taxes owed and taxes paid. Taxes paid account for deductions, tax credits, exemptions, and deferrals. That's the value of tax professionals – to keep track of these things. Income, real estate, business, and sales tax are all a primary expense for most households but maybe under the radar in the $100,000-$300,000 household income range.

Question: Do you know how much in overall taxes (income, real estate, business, and sales) your household pays?

Generally speaking, most people don't. There are plenty of discussions on how different governments use federal, state, and local taxes. For now, we'll put **how the government chooses to spend tax dollars** into the "little or no control" bucket for our partnership money conversations. But as you start to move higher up the income brackets, taxes become more significant.

We also make an assumption related to taxes: that your goal is to minimize taxes. We use those words carefully from the standpoint of not attempting to avoid taxes. That's illegal. You can pay taxes now, or you pay taxes later, but Uncle Sam— or, depending on your state, Aunt Washington— are both part of your financial picture.

Question: Do you know the difference between your marginal tax rate and your effective tax rate? You don't pay your highest income tax level on all of your income. It's a little nuance, but it could affect your decisions, and coordinating these efforts between taxes and your income in retirement does require a little more than just notes on the back of the napkin. So you want to be careful.

Question: Do you understand the difference between a tax deduction and a tax credit? Generally, a tax deduction can reduce your taxable income. Generally, a tax credit can reduce your tax amount owed. They are different.

Also, some deductions can be applied regardless of whether you decide to take the standard deduction or itemize deductions, and some deductions can only apply to itemize deductions. Tax rules and laws periodically change, so strategies need to adjust to these rules. Please be careful of these pseudo-tax experts who offer free tax advice – especially on social media. Free advice can often fall into the "it depends" category. Last time I checked, not everybody ran to their CPA or their enrolled agent to help them make decisions.

Questions: Do you proactively reach out to a CPA regarding your partnership decisions regarding a home purchase, or starting or running a business? If you have an investment professional, do you coordinate with your CPA?

One last word on taxes, as our world tries to recover from the COVID-19 pandemic. Since March of 2020, there have been significant fiscal adjustments to navigate the pandemic's impact on households and businesses. In line with the concept of no free lunch, taxes are likely to rise to pay for services currently provided in my propinion. How will tax increases affect your household going forward? What is within your control regarding the impact taxes have on your goals?

Inflation

We have to consider inflation, too. Inflation is the doppelganger of the compounding effect: Instead of working for you, inflation eats away at asset values and raises your expenses in the future. To level-set, inflation is the change in the price of the same good or services, usually measured yearly.

Academically, most people use the CPI (Consumer Price Index) number to approximate inflation, but actual inflation depends on what you spend money on and your assets.

Here's an example, using the value and goal of higher education that many of you have for your family. In 1998, someone set aside $100,000 for their child; the same year I started my career. The purpose of the $100,00 was to A) fully fund public college education including room, board, and tuition; or B) fully fund four-year tuition at a private school.

Another value is to assist with the cost of purchasing a home for adult children. The $100,000 could be: C) a major contribution toward the purchase of an average-priced home. Fast forward 20 years to 2018. That same $100,000 without any growth in 2018 does not realistically meet the education mentioned above goals. And depending on your location, it doesn't even provide a 20% down payment on an average house (at least in Seattle).

In a single generation, inflation can double the price of things we need or want, or halve the purchasing power of the money we have. The horseman of inflation has decimated many long-term financial plans and should be factored in—even in the intermediate timeframe.

Also, we need to calculate for some inflation regarding the impact on Social Security and Medicare. Your assignment *—and you thought there wasn't any homework* - is to relate longevity, taxes, and inflation to your overall Do-What-You-Want goals.

Healthcare

To have better conversations and make better decisions now, so you can Do-What-You-Want later, come in prepared with data. Honestly, this section was a little tough to put together due to laws' fluidity, changing costs, and, frankly, the landscape can be a downer. But this guide isn't just about puppy dogs and ice-cream. Healthcare is a real horseman.

We'll use long-term healthcare costs as one aspect of healthcare. Still, these questions also apply to rising costs (inflation), medication, hearing, vision, dental, and some high-income surcharges for high-income earners.

"Long-term care involves a variety of services designed to meet a person's health or personal care needs during a short or longer period, as you will see. These services help people live as independently and safely as possible when they can no longer perform everyday activities on their own." [National Institute of Mental Health. (2018)]

Hopefully, your retirement will involve years of travel, hobbies, and fulfilling activities. However, if you live long enough, you likely will need some level of care eventually, and this care will be more involved and expensive as we age. Most retirees want to maintain as much independence as possible for as long as possible, so let's say you just have someone come in for simple housekeeping tasks. That will set you back, on average, $21 an hour. [Genworth. (2017)] Not too bad. However, as care gets more involved, the cost goes up. A lot. Residing in an assisted living facility (ALF) costs, on average, $3,750 a month, even though the care provided is generally not as "extensive as that of a nursing home." [Genworth. (2017)]. An average nursing home is steeper, coming in at $235 a day on average for a semi-private room, or $7,050 for a thirty-day stay. [Genworth. (2017)]. Considering that "Half of all older adults had less than $25,601 in yearly income from all sources" in 2019, its clear that planning for healthcare in retirement needs to happen well in advance. [Pension Rights Center. (n.d.)]

Another consideration is who will provide your care. Caregivers can be paid (formal) or unpaid (informal). Unpaid caregivers are often family members. While being cared for in old age by a family member may sound better personally and economically, many unpaid caregivers experience negative professional consequences resulting from their caregiving duties. In fact, "70% of working caregivers suffer work-related difficulties due to their dual roles" as employees and unpaid caregivers. [Genworth. (2017)]. Unpaid caregivers, because of their connection to their charge(s), often feel a strong sense of obligation. These caregivers may very well be your adult children or other relatives. Ideally, you'll retire with funds set aside to compensate your caregiver, even if that person is a relative. This could provide them with the flexibility to reduce their work hours, take a less stressful job, or otherwise alter their employment to better coordinate with their caregiver duties.

One source I found helpful as a starting point for healthcare statistics is Christina Benz's Morningstar article "75 Must-Know Statistics About Long-Term Care: 2018 Edition"

Questions:

How likely are you two to need long-term care, and for how long?
What does long-term care cost - overall?
What does it cost to insure against it?

Do-What-You-Want:
My Little Ponies

After the four horsemen, we don't want to completely discount the "little ponies" of retirement. Earlier in the "What Do You Have" section, we outlined different liabilities, including student loans and mortgages. They both carry their unique characteristics and challenges. In the "Vehicles" section, we highlight how annuities - as a vehicle and a process- address converting a single dollar amount into a stream of payments. Here we will highlight the other two ponies: variable income and family dynamics and overview retirement platforms.

Variable Income

Historically, our job and career paths were linear, and generally stable. For some of us, our incomes changes with life events. If the company is doing well, you may feel overly confident in your future level of income. I've learned - never underestimate the ability of a company to change its direction overnight. Your income may vary more than you think in future.

Here's my personal story. I started my career in 1998 with Salomon Smith Barney, a company owned by the firm Citigroup Inc., which, at the time, was the largest financial institution in the world. Salomon Smith Barney was Citigroup's brokerage house unit. I cut my teeth on wealth management within a unit of Smith Barney called the Consulting Group, which focused on providing fiduciary investment advice.

By 2008, I completed ten years with Citigroup, and my compensation was a mixture of base salary, bonuses paid in cash and stock, and a portion held back for future distribution. Things weren't looking bad. That all changed in 2008. We've all heard the stories about what happened to Bear Sterns and Lehman Brothers, but the whole financial community was changed.

The largest institution in the world owned Smith Barney, so we were safe, right? In one weekend, it was assumed Citigroup would purchase Wells Fargo/Wachovia, and the next week Citigroup was sold to Morgan Stanley. But more importantly, the stock prices plummeted. One detail about our compensation: a portion of our bonus was deferred and highly dependent on stock prices. Shares of Citigroup Inc., once the nation's most powerful bank, went from $27.35 per share April 28th, 2007 to $.97 per share just one year later on April 28th, 2008. That a 95.56% decline.

The good news: I was still in the early stage (early 30s) of my career. Ten years of receiving a certain percentage of my income in company stock did impact my overall net worth, but it wasn't a game-changer. Other older employees and had a majority of their net worth tied to company stock weren't so lucky. Unfortunately, I even knew a financial advisor who took his life because of all the chaos the 2008 financial crisis created. Some co-workers made an active decision to concentrate their stock in one position, and those people paid dearly.

The moral of the story: For those whose income includes company stock as a form of compensation, beware of the risk. Yes, you can amass a significant amount of wealth. Also, note that I've worked for firms that offer stock option plans to technology companies, so I'm familiar with how company stock affects overall net worth in a very positive way. But if you were to tell me in April 2007 that the transaction fee at an ATM would cost more than buying a share of stock my company, I would have never believed you.

As in "The Three Little Pigs," it never hurts to pick up some mortaring skills because you never know when the Big Bad Wolf (financial storm) is coming. How are you balancing the growth potential of company stock versus the risk of a single stock risk?

Variable income is not just about losing stock options. Traditional financial planning models assume inflation adjustments to income. Still, real-life includes periods of reduced compensation through missed bonuses, changing roles due to company restructuring, and time off due to family – this can include the birth of a child and taking care of loved ones, starting a business, going back to school, and general poor employment prospects. The good news is that two potential incomes can provide stability over a single source, all else being equal.

Questions:
- What are your career plans with your current job?
- How do you treat additional income above your salary or hourly wage?
- What reserve funds have you set aside for goals like additional schooling or starting a business?

Family Dynamics

What do I mean by family dynamics? Family dynamics include the positive and negative effects of family members (outside of your partner) that affect your decision making. Let's assume that someone's parents have not adequately planned for their retirement. They have not saved enough for retirement, and they cannot afford to live their lifestyle on their own; they will run out of money in the first 3-5 years in retirement. They need help with their living expenses.

If a person or partnership place "family" high on their values list--and most people would include their parents as part of the family— how is that reflected in their life? In practice, which do they rate higher: family or independence? Do they offer help with TEAM resources? Or do they sit on the sideline and watch it play out?

I've had enough people in my financial planning practice describe a situation where there was a disconnect. A fallacy is they will simply "figure it out." In other words, if someone lives a $125,000 yearly expense lifestyle, but they only bring in $50,000 in income, they will see the deficit (mind the gap), and they will adjust accordingly? My experience is that people are not always self-correcting in the short term – especially later in life. Maybe someone has done the research, but my experience is that there's about a 50/50 chance that they will change their behavior (spending patterns) to match their new income. Like a doctor assessing a patient—we are not blaming them, it's merely an observation—a common statement I hear is, "I did X, Y, and Z (fill in the blank of what they did), *therefore, I deserve this lifestyle.*"

If family members don't change their spending, they will hopefully find some alternatives to retiring. Some levels of discomfort are not optimal, but at some level, it will work. I always joke (tongue in cheek) that my in-laws may never need me, but I should be nice because *I* may need *them.* We'll talk about "mind the gap" later, and it's surprising how many people aren't where they want to be in retirement. It's not homeless vs. paradise lifestyle conversation, but many people are somewhere in the middle.

Here's the rub. *Who* is going to tell them? As a financial advisor, you are always aware that bad news leads to accounts transferring and clients asking for a 2nd opinion from someone who will tell them the answer they are looking for. Later we will note how well adult children listen to their parents, but in their later years, *parents don't always respond to guidance from children and others*; –and, yes, financial professionals are others.

Someone reading this might think, "My mother and father are in good health." Yes, they are for now, but these things can spring upon us like a pop quiz our sophomore year of geometry. Cognitive skills can decline without warning, and important decisions are left to those who are unprepared. Sometimes we just aren't ready.

On the other side, let's say you or your partner has a relative that doesn't have kids or other beneficiaries. And she has plans to leave her legacy by bequeathing property, her IRA, stock, or even proceeds from a life insurance policy to you. She could set aside funds for higher education during her living years. This is the positive side of family dynamics. Your partnership can benefit from incorporating family members by blood or relations into your decisions regarding resource allocation. These are next "next level" conversations.

Questions:
Have you spoken to your parents about their retirement needs/wants?
How would you describe your lines of communication regarding financial matters with family members?
What are the expectations for them living in their later years?
Are the thoughts and concerns of both partners communicated to their parents?
Do parents have a living trust, financial Power of Attorney (P.O.A.), healthcare POA, and health care directive?
Are there siblings that may need extra attention in their adult life?
How do you factor in a sibling that needs TEAM resources based on your partnership's values?
How do blood relatives communicate partnership TEAM resources to their partner regarding non-blood-related relatives?
Are relatives a resource for financial support - even in a lending capacity?
Is there an unspoken expectation of repayment for previous support, financial or otherwise?

Income-Replacement Needs in Retirement

Many of the concepts and discussions in *Marriage & Money* are directed toward average-sized households related to income. A fundamental question for all partners reading this is: How much will we need in retirement? We can think of the need as a lump sum –one number– or as annual income to last *both partners*' lifetime. There are other factors, so this is just meant to give you something to think, discuss, and, ultimately, move forward related to your personal information. Again, this is to illustrate a point.

Let's say two individuals each make an average individual income amount. In Seattle, that is roughly $75,000 a year. If you put them together, you now have a household income of $150,000. Let's address the fundamental question: How much annual income (replacement) would this household need in retirement before accounting for inflation and other factors? No, I didn't pull this question from a GMAT test.   This is real life. Remember, $100,000-$150,000 annualized income is representative of a group that, in my opinion, is often neglected when we talk about average-sized households.

Suppose you were to retire tomorrow, with a household income of $150,000. How much annual income will you require to continue in the same lifestyle within retirement, not considering the number of years in retirement? The quick takeaway, based on this example: it's about 75%. [GTR 2020]

Here's how we get to that number: First, we assume a household will need to put about 6% less money in savings because you've already retired. Second, you're lowering your expenditures by about 8%. When you're not working, your transportation, clothing, and other costs drop. And third, you're looking at lower taxes—about 11% lower—which makes sense. You're making less, spending less, and your income is less, so you're taxed less.

But that still leaves about 75% of $150,000. Of the 75%, we assume roughly 25% should is covered by Social Security benefits. So then you'll need to make up about $75,000 a year or so. That can come from a 401(k), a pension, a home sale, or another source. Regardless, you will want to find a source to replace that income.

Relate that number to one of the four horsemen, longevity, and tie in a minor but significant factor – converting a lump sum into a stream of income with a level of certainty for an unknown longevity period. Let's just use raw numbers over a 20-year window. Let's say Social Security has been maxed out. In this example, the partnership will need $75,000 a year for 20 years, for $1,500,000 over that period, not accounting for inflation, growth of retirement funds, or other factors.

Back to our discussion of millionaires from the "What You Have" section. You would need another 50% more than your $1,000,000 goal to maintain your lifestyle. Many people in my parents' generation alluded to needing one million dollars to retire. That was 20 years ago. For many reading this, retirement is at least another 20-40 years away from today. Retiring at today's cost could very well increase due to inflation.

This is in no way a complete exercise of your retirement needs. Just consider this book a source of references for educational purposes only, to help you have better money conversations and make better decisions.

If you ask, "How long should we plan for our retirement?" based on the longevity numbers we've already discussed, some may want to use 20 years as a starting point. As a reminder, longevity is based on multiple factors – some are out of your control, but you don't want to screw this number up. You don't want to get to age 75 and realize you messed up your calculations. (Or have your family or caregiver realize it for you.) Because then you'll find yourself or partnership in a position where you, or someone caring for you, is going to have to make some tough choices on your behalf. I'm not saying your kids are going to take you on a "vacation" and then "forget" you somewhere … But it could get tricky.

I'm also not implying that everyone will be destitute and on the streets by their seventh year of retirement. But if your calculations are off, you may have to start selling off assets you want to keep, or you may have to figure out some other way to get income—a stressful proposition. You might not be able to leave the legacy you planned because assets didn't last as long as needed.

Some groups— HENRYs —may think this doesn't apply to them because of their high income. These concerns aren't restricted to lower-income folks or people who are at the margins. Even those who are on pace to what most people consider significant assets—a million dollars—or earn an annual income in the range of $150,000 to $300,000, may not saving enough to make the reality of retirement match the picture their heads.

Because when you raise your level of income, you also typically raise the level of your lifestyle. Remember: **It's not how much you make; it's how much you keep**. And that's a whole different conversation to have: the lifestyle people expect to live in the Do-What-You-Want period concerning their circumstances now. Aligning the resources that go along with an extended elevated lifestyle takes some work.

Retirement Plans

Employer-Sponsored Retirement Plans:

Here a list of the most common employer-sponsored retirement plans: Simplified Employment Pension (SEP) (tax advantage plans), SIMPLE IRAs, 401(k) regulars, profit-sharing plans, Money Purchases, Target Benefit Plans, Saving/Match or Thrift Plans, Stock Bonus Plans, Employee Stock Ownership Plans (ESOP), Traditional Defined Benefit Plans, and Cash Balance Pension Plans.

Traditional Defined Benefit Plans or Pension plans are great for employees because they create a consistent stream of income in the future. Not many companies offer pension plans as they are a significant liability for the company, but when available, pension plans help address the challenge of converting a lump sum into a stream of payments.

Tax-Advantaged Plans – Individuals
Individual Retirement Accounts (IRA):
Traditional IRA, and Roth I.R.A., Solo Roth

403(b) for employees of non-profits, tax-exempt businesses—think schools, universities, churches and religious organizations, or hospitals.

457 plans are for local and state government employees like the local police and fire department. Generally speaking, these plans allow deferral of income tax.

A Health Savings Account (HSA) is a tax-advantaged account created for individuals who are covered under high-deductible health plans (HDHPs) to save (pretax money) for qualified medical expenses beyond HDHPs coverage limits and exclusions.

The Roth feature takes **after-tax** dollars and allows for tax-free growth and withdrawals if rules are met. They are offered in an IRA, 401(k), 403(b), or 457 options.

Which plan is right for you?
If you are not the employer – the right plan is one that is offered through your job. If not, you may want to consult a retirement specialist regarding your options.

What questions should you ask?
- When am I eligible to participate? (This is otherwise known as vesting.)
- Can my employer contribute? If so, by rule or by choice? How much per year?
- What is the maximum salary deferral? (Defer refers to tax treatment.)
- If you are over age 50, is there a catch-up provision? If so, how much?
- What are the rules regarding loans, withdrawals, and repayment?
- What is the annual salary limit, and how does it apply?

*Remember to address adding the appropriate party (your partner) as a beneficiary to these accounts.

Risk & Return

"I'd rather be vaguely right than precisely wrong." – John Maynard Keynes

When it comes to any investment, the number one factor we focus on is the return. At the most basic level, will I have more at the end of the period than what I started with? If you invest $100 at beginning of a period and at the end of the period you have $107, that's a 7% return. Let's go a little deeper.

The Power of Compounding: "Money Makes Money"

You may have heard the phrase "compounded returns." This is one of the secret ingredients for successful investing.

Let's look at putting away $4,000 a year and earning 7% each year and retiring at age 66.

Start investing at age 21 – total at retirement $1,142,997
Start investing at age 31 – total at retirement $552,948
Start investing at age 41 – total at retirement $252,996

If you put away $4,000 every year starting at age 21, and that money returns 7% a year, in 45 years—when you're age 66—you'll have a little bit over a million dollars. It's true – the numbers don't lie. One million dollars from tucking away about $350/month, or just under $100 a week. Now let's say you wait until age 31 to get started. That not a huge deal, right? Wrong. Your compounding power drops in HALF – a significant loss of return. And let's just say you start at 41 and you want to retire at sixty-five. That compounding has even less of an effect and less time to grow over just 25 years versus 45 years. You're contributing the same dollar amount, and you get the same rate of return, but it's over a much shorter period, so you don't get the growth on the growth for nearly as long.

What does "growth on the growth" mean? Although you're just putting in that $4,000 every year, you aren't making 7% on just that $4,000 as you keep going—you're also making 7% on the *gains* over time. For example, after year one, you'd have $280 extra in return for a total of $4,280. The following year, even if you didn't add anything else, your return would amount to almost $300, because it isn't a 7% rate of return (in this example) on just $4,000 anymore—it's 7% on $4,280. The following year—again, still without adding anything else, the return: $320.

And when you keep adding your $4,000 to the amount each year, it grows even faster. That's the power of compounding—that is what "money makes money" means.

Starting late?

Investing $10,000 a year at age 51 and earning 15% each year and retiring at age 66.   Total is only $475,804.

Even if you put a lot away later because you think you'll play catch-up, and even if you double the return from 7% to 15%, it is still harder to catch up than if you had just started 15 or 20 years earlier. Why? Because you're getting just 15 or 20 years of compounding versus 35, 40, or more. The verb (investing) creates the noun (investments).

I know this takes a lot of effort. I know it takes sacrifices to pull this off—compound returns matter. To get them, you have to *save* and *invest*. If you *"live only for today"* and discount the future, your future will be discounted—and it arrives faster than you think.

Winning by Not Losing

Returns aren't always positive; however—nearly everyone who invests will experience gains and losses. And losses are hard to overcome, in part because the math seems almost unfair.

Here's an example. You invest $1, and it loses 50% in the first year but then gains 50% on that amount in the second year. No problem, you're back to even, right? Not quite.

After your first year, you have $.50 left from your original $1. At that point, a 50% gain in year two means you have $.75 —you're not back to your full dollar yet. It works the same in reverse, too. If you gain 50% in year one, you have $1.50 by year end. But when you lose 50% in year two, you're at $.75, just like the first scenario. So while it might sound obvious to say, "the less you lose, the more you win," minimizing losses can make a big difference in your long-term returns.

Return vs. Performance

It's important to understand two basic concepts as you move forward: return and performance. Return is the example we illustrated earlier. It's a number – in our compounding example earlier, it was 7%. It's simply the difference of the ending value and the beginning value, divided by the beginning value. The return is a raw number.

Return Calculation

$$\frac{\text{Difference between Starting Value - Ending Value}}{\text{Starting Value}}$$

Performance is different because it is the return in relation to your expectation. If we are looking at returns that already occurred—let's use our 7%—is that good or bad? Remember our assumption from the introduction: It depends. If your investment returned 7% in 1999, that means it vastly underperformed the overall stock market. It would also depend on which asset class was at stake: cash, bond, or stock. It would also depend on the sector, such as technology or manufacturing. Performance is in the eye of the beholder. As a partnership, you will want to look through the same monocles.

Your frame of reference also matters. Let's say you invest $1,000 on January 1st with your investment professional, and it is worth $1,400 on April 30th. However, it doesn't do much for the rest of the year, dropping slightly from its high and ending up at $1,250. How would you describe your performance? If you ask a financial advisor, they would tell you the annual return was 25%, which certainly sounds good. However, you might think of that 25% as a defeat, given you were sitting with a 40% return at one point. It all depends on your frame of reference.

Advanced Returns

Every once in a while, I'll listen to a talk radio show or conversations online about "returns that don't make sense." Let's say at the beginning of the year; you invest $1,000 in the stock market. At the end of the first year, you've done well, and the portfolio is now worth $1,200. So you've made $200 on your $1,000 or 20%. Now, you have this stock market "thing" figured out, you decide to put $100,000 into the stock market. Then in year two, we make the same $200. What is your overall return? Well, it's not so clear now—we can't just use the equation from before, ending value minus beginning value, divided by beginning value, because the massive contribution in year two would throw things out of whack.

Beginning value:	$1,000
End value:	$101,400

If you don't account for the $100,000 you added to the account after year one, the return is going to look massive, and someone is looking like an all-star investor. Let's slow down.

Two factors affect your gain or loss —the investment losses or gains based on the market performance and decisions related to the advisor and the investment value added or subtracted based on the client's decision.

And it works the other way too. I had two clients who, after a period of investing with me, decided to buy a house with the funds from their investment account. So if we used the simple return calculation, we would have a substantial negative return. I think most people understand that a financial advisor does not have any control over the client taking money out of their portfolio. The return in that instance—at least the "return" looking at the total account value, without adjusting for the client's decision—was not a reflection of the advisor's ability.

That's why we have a dollar-weighted return, which measures what happened during the period in terms of the amount in the account or portfolio. And a time-weighted return, which tries to more accurately reflect returns by isolating the market's effect or investment performance on the portfolio.

The takeaway: If you ever have a portfolio return that doesn't seem to make sense, there is a likelihood the calculation is averaging out or negating the effect of your decision to add or subtract money.

Why does this matter? Every return with a large inflow or outflow relative to the size of the initial investment will affect the return. The closer it is to the end or beginning of the period, the more significant the effect. In general, you want to separate your additions and subtractions to an investment account from the investments themselves' market returns. Otherwise, you might find that you think your returns are better (or worse) than they are. Know what you are measuring.

Risk: Deep-Fried Turkey

When I say "risk," many people immediately think of insurance— or maybe skydiving, riding a motorcycle, or some other dangerous activity. Risk is simply "exposure to danger, harm or loss," but it comes in many different flavors. And it's not black or white; it's not a matter of either accepting risk or eliminating it. It's important to evaluate all of your options, which may include mitigating risk in some way.

For example, have you ever deep-fried a turkey? If you haven't tried it, you should, because it's delicious. Imagine taking this large bird and, instead of shoving it into an oven, you drop it into a vat of hot oil. Here are four scenarios regarding deep-frying a turkey. First, if you deep-fry a turkey in your kitchen and aren't careful, there's a real risk that you'll cause damage to yourself and your home. Every year, you hear stories about people destroying their kitchen, or even burning down their house, while deep-frying a turkey. But if you go through with it, knowing the risk ahead of time, that's what we call "assuming the risk."

Or You're a little smarter and take the operation out to the garage or backyard, where it's a lot safer—at least if you start a fire, it won't destroy your home. There's still a chance you could damage your property, but now you're "reducing the risk."

You might think, "I'm even smarter than that. I'm going to take this production over to my cousin's house." We call this third option "transferring the risk."

Finally, you can roast your turkey in the oven the old-fashioned way, or celebrate Thanksgiving at a restaurant, thereby "eliminating the risk" of a deep-fryer fire. (But note that you're not eliminating the risk that your oven could catch on fire!)

Key Point: Evaluate your options and the risk each carries. Look at how your decision affects the overall picture. Identify the risks and the options on how best to mitigate those risks.

Risk in Investments—Variability

When we talk about your investments' risk level, the goal is to manage that risk by not putting all your eggs in one basket. When you invest, you expect a return on that investment. Let's say you have $100 to invest in ABC stock. I tell you that your money should earn 10% annually. So if you give me $100, you'll expect to have $110 at the end of a year. That's a 10% return.

But that outcome is only a reasonable hope. There's also some risk involved. And that risk is that the actual return is frequently different than the expected return. Your stock, worth $100 initially, could be valued at the end of any given year at $140. Or it may be worth $84. That difference between the measured average return (multiple returns measured over multiple periods) and the actual return in any given year is the variability. Usually, stock market returns do not move in a straight line. With variability, in any specific year the price goes up and down, and our expectation of 10% is an *average outcome.*

How many times do you hear the stock market averages 7%-9% over the long term?

Myth: You should expect 7-9% returns – every year.

Reality: Since 1923, the S&P 500 Index has rarely returned between 7%-9% measured by annualized returns.

Are the personal finance experts wrong? No, they're just not putting returns in relation to the variability of returns that produce the quoted average.

Don't try to walk across a river that is four feet deep <u>on average</u> but has a section that is 10 feet deep if you can't swim.

The more confident you are that you're going to receive a return, the more valuable that investment is — typically.

The value we give the actual investment product is based on what we expect AND the probability that it will happen. Some people look at investment risk in terms of, "Am I going to get my money back? Or could it go to zero?" But that's not the only way you measure investment risk. Whether it's your house, your 401(k), or something else, you want to look at them in terms of their current investment value, expected value in the future with a probability, and risk profile.

Fast Car

As 15-year-olds, my friends and I would walk past the local car lot and talk about the cars we would have when we turned 16. At that point, we all played sports; thus, no employment, AND we had a 15-year old's criteria for selecting cars. Our process as 15-year old's was:

> #1 price (the amount we were asking our parents for)
> #2 color (black and metallic grey)
> #3 how quickly it went from 0 to 60 mph.

That was at age 15, and since then, my criteria have changed – a back-up camera is a must.

When you look at investments, consider more than just the upside, the 0-60 mph stat, as it were. Regarding investment returns, it's not only about the potential upside; it's about the ability to achieve a return with a certain level of consistency and, thus, *confidence*.

If you normally glide over the disclaimers -let me tell you why this is important. Warnings should be carefully noted: "items in the side-view mirror may be closer than they appear" or "cotton shrinks when washed in hot water." Don't overlook disclaimers concerning past investment performance. Because at any given time, the market has a right, and sometimes an obligation, to make a move you weren't expecting. In other words, there is a chance that you may lose money. Which leads me to a favorite saying when things don't go as planned with the stock market: "I'm disappointed, but not surprised."

Peanut Butter and Jelly

For about 40 years, I've loved eating peanut butter and jelly sandwiches. And I can't just have a peanut butter sandwich, the sandwich *needs* jelly. The same applies to risk and reward. You may evaluate an investment vehicle, and you want to take only the best part, the upside: the peanut butter. But the investment comes with another ingredient: the jelly. That is the concept of risk and return. They stick together, and you can't have one without the other. My apologies to those who can't eat or don't like peanut butter.

It helps explain the concept of "no free lunch." Most decisions have a pro and a con to them. When you make decisions, and you don't see the downside: be cautious because unforeseen roadblocks and obstacles can derail plans. Evaluate all the differences in all the return opportunities and probabilities and understand what it takes to achieve those goals.

Generally speaking:

More risk, more return.

Less risk, less return.

*When you hear "risk-free" related to investing or a business opportunity– be very, very cautious. Generally speaking, there is no free lunch.

Diversification: Cooking with Investments

If you look back in history, you can see how evaluating investments evolved. In the middle of the 20th century, Harry Markowitz revolutionized the investment world with his investment evaluation findings. At the time, everyone else was evaluating portfolios by two measurements: risk and return. Markowitz noted a third factor, called correlation, that essentially measured how each investment moves with other investments. This third factor, along with risk and return, impacted how investments were viewed. His modern portfolio theory essentially blew the collective financial community's mind and won him a Nobel Prize in 1990. [Markowitz, H. (1952)] While the mechanics of modern portfolio theory are advanced, in practice, we use similar concepts every day.

My family is from the South, and my mother was raised in New Orleans. Our family makes gumbo every major holiday. Like every family dish, gumbo has the basic recipe, and then it has the *secret* ingredient. But it's not just the secret ingredient that makes the difference—**it's how it's added in combination with everything else.**

In my family, the secret ingredient is okra — I think. Many people aren't crazy about okra as a standalone vegetable; however, by some standards, when you add okra to gumbo, it transforms the overall flavor and experience—it adds that "special something" to it. In this case, a specific investment may seem dull or lackluster at face value. Still, when included with other non-correlated investments, it can reduce the investment portfolio risk and may even increase the return overall.

To further the analogy, some would say that adding something like hot sauce to gumbo would make it too spicy for anybody under the age of 2 or over the age of 85. But Harry Markowitz's modern portfolio theory would endorse the addition, saying that adding the right amount of hot sauce, relative to the other ingredients, diminishes its overwhelming effect while enriching the mix. In the case of investments, adding an asset that is riskier than the overall portfolio can actually reduce the overall risk based on how it moves with other investments in the portfolio.

Have you ever noticed a person with a nice business suit, but when you look at the shoes, you can only think, "Oh no!!!" The kids today say, "What ARE those?!!!" Wrong combination.

To recap, it's a combination of the expected return, the expected risk, and the correlation. These are the tenets of modern portfolio theory. And whether you're working with an investment professional or evaluating things on your own, it can help you determine whether an investment makes sense to consider overall.

The Importance of Diversification

When you diversify your investments, you reduce your risk of catastrophic loss. Let's look at that ABC stock example. If your entire nest egg is in ABC stock, and ABC stock plummets, there goes your nest egg.

Now, say instead that you put half of your nest egg in ABC stock and the other half in another investment. If ABC stock plummets, but the other investment remains steady, your nest egg is in much better shape than it was in the other scenario—because you've spread your risk. By smoothing out the volatility, you can protect your portfolio as a whole. You also can improve your long-term performance because not losing (or not losing as much) makes it much easier to win.

That's the ultimate goal of modern portfolio diversification—creating the best possible combination of stocks or other assets, based on the expected returns and the expected volatility, or fluctuations, of those returns over time.

The benefits of diversification go far beyond that. The returns on different assets usually are not strictly correlated — in other words, they don't always move up or down in lockstep. This means the returns on the assets in a diversified portfolio are likely to offset each other, at least in part. Diversification reduces the overall volatility of returns, which is a crucial measure of investment risk. Generally speaking: Lower volatility can lead to faster compounding over time, thus improving your overall returns.

Your Shield, Your Sword, and Your Boots

Let's look at three different kinds of investments: stocks, bonds, and cash. Stocks are simply ownership in a company—if you own a company's share, you literally own part of the company.

- When an investor buys a bond, the investors are loaning money to a company (private) or governmental (public) entity, which borrows that money for a defined period and pays interest.

- And then the cash is just that: cash.

We're going to start with stocks. This analogy is a gross generalization, but there's a large segment of millennials who do not own stocks or invest in the stock market. For some, it might not matter. But for many of them, investing in stocks would provide the returns needed to reach their goals.

When a co-worker at JP Morgan was asked, "Why should I invest in stocks?" he would say, "Stocks are your sword." You use them to move forward, to make gains, to achieve goals. You want to try to take advantage of those opportunities in the market that'll help you meet your goals.

The problem with stocks is that, on an individual basis, it's possible they could crash, even all the way down to zero, on any given day. The probability may not be high, but the possibility is there. You can lose a significant amount of money in a short time. So what can you do? As we talked about earlier, you can invest in more than one stock—diversify.

By investing in more than one stock, different industries, different sizes, and even in different countries, you reduce the risk (like deep-frying your turkey in the back yard versus the kitchen). One stock might go down, but chances are the other stocks won't move in precisely the same direction at the same magnitude. Once you get past a certain number of stocks—say, 30 to 40—you don't experience as much risk reduction by adding more stocks.

Regarding reducing risk, you are better off with a basket of stocks rather than when you owned just that one stock - generally speaking. If you're like many people, you don't want just stocks because stocks are volatile. So you add another investment— what is often called a fixed-income investment, like bonds.

Note: (fixed-income, debt, bonds are generally describing the same thing)

Bonds are your shield. In theory, when the stock market goes down, people invest in bonds, and then the demand drives the price of the bonds up. Generally speaking, there is an inverse activity when you compare these two vehicles' performance—when one goes up, the other often goes down, but not always. (Warning: I'm pulling out my "it depends" card; there are other factors that affect the price of bonds, like fiscal and monetary policy and general supply-demand in the open market place, to name a few.) Then again, if you invest solely in the safety of bonds, your chances of reaching your goals are lower – generally speaking, compared to a mixture of stocks and bonds. You might see steady movement, steady gains, but those gains are smaller than the potential gains with stocks.

It's also important to keep in mind that fixed-income investments like these can drop when interest rates go up. For example, if you buy a bond that pays 5% and interest rates go to 7%, someone who buys a bond at 7% can better return. This means your 5% bond is less valuable than that 7% new bond - in this example.

Finally, you've got some cash. Cash are your boots. That's what helps you get out of Dodge, whether you need to move from one asset class to another, or find safety. "Safe" is a relative term, though, because of inflation. If you keep $1,000 under your bed for five years, you'll still have $1,000 at the end—but that $1,000 likely won't buy nearly as much as it would today.

Winning Takes the Right Mix

You probably need equities, your sword, to achieve your goals. Fixed income, your shield, can help you protect yourself by reducing your exposure to market swings. And cash, your boots, gives you the ability to make moves and remove investment risk altogether– even though you still have a loss of purchasing power.

The mix is what reduces the movement, or the volatility. That's important because volatility can make us do strange things—things that can sabotage our goals.

A famous financial study conducted by Brinson, Beebower, & Hood in 1986 found the number one factor of your investing success is the movement created by your mix of stocks, bonds, and cash. In other words, the movement created by stocks can cause you to become "scared" and pull your money out. [Brinson, Beebower, and Hood (1986)] But that's what people do—when the market makes big swings, they sell to take profits or sell because they've already lost value and don't want to lose more.

We saw that in 2008. People who had a portfolio at that time will tell you all about it. "I lost most of my money." But every once in a while, you have an "all-star" who will tell you, "I saw it coming and got my money out."

Ok, so they got out. Great, right? After all, the S&P 500 was down nearly 40% for 2008. But when did they get out? When they were already down 10%? 20%? And when did they get back in? If they're honest, many waited until the dust settled. And they missed a lot of the steady climb back—the very next year 2009, the S&P 500 gained about 25%. By the end of 2013, the index was 25% higher than it was *before* the recession.

Trying to time the market can be difficult and potentially costly. Too often, instead of buying low and selling high, people freak out when the market drops and sell. Then, the recovery begins, and they wait, the recovery completes, and then they buy back in. That's selling low *and* buying high!

And even if you get out of the stock market at the right time, you really can't STAY out because cash alone doesn't achieve much. It's just your boots for moving around the battlefield, remember? It's tough to march to any kind of victory without a sword and a shield.

Beat the Market

You have probably heard the statement, "You can't beat the market." I put that in the category of that may or may not be true, but you're focusing on the wrong things.

Nothing illustrated this more than when I was at a networking mixer early in 2018. When I introduce myself as a financial planner, there are typically three reactions:

1) a blank look, as in *"I have no idea what that mea*ns."

2) *"Oh, I probably need one of those,"* and they ask me questions related to their personal situation - which is fine. <u>But every once in a while</u>, I receive the third response.

3) Someone trying to prove how smart they are at my expense. In this situation, this guy was relatively new to the insurance industry -less than two years would be my guess. He treated financial planning and insurance sales as a competition. To be clear, I think these are two separate and complementary roles.

Here's the story: We were at a table of five people, and I'm responding to a financial planning question from someone in the beauty care industry. The insurance guy cut into our 1:1 conversation as I'm leaving my card with the other business owner. I don't remember his exact words, but as I start to turn and walk away, the guy comments, *"Why are you asking him? He can't even beat the market."* Implying that my recommendation of investments would not return more than the stock market.

And everybody kind of looks at me, like, "*Challenge.*"

Later, I'll talk about managing emotions – this is one. I start to walk away and, like a salmon hooked on a line, I feel compelled to just make sure he had the correct information. So I turn around and look at him, and simply respond, "*I don't think you understand the question you asked.*"

We exchange looks, but without further incident, we part ways.

Have you ever thought about how you could have responded differently to someone acting "less than cordially" after the fact? Mine would have looked like this:

Me: Look, I don't think you understand the question you asked.

Him: What? It's a pretty simple question. Can. You. Beat. The. Market? You either can or can't, it's pretty straight forward, you do, or you don't."

Me: Again, let me state: I don't think you understand the question you asked, but since you're asking, do you mind if I gather a bit more information to help you out?

I know he thinks I'm about to launch into an investment product pitch.

Him: (arms folded) Please.

Me: *Which market are you talking about?*

Him: The stock market.

Me: *Sure, the stock market, but the Dow Jones Industrial Average? The Standard & Poor's 500 Index? or Russell 1000 or 3000?- which one?*

Him: Well, you know, S&P 500. Let's start with the largest 500 companies.

Me: Not necessarily. The S&P 500 index has a committee to decide who to include/exclude based on other factors beyond market capitalization or size. * liquidity, industry representation in the US economy, and financial viability.

Him: Yeah, I mean the Dow Jones Industrial Average - works just as well. They're all pretty much the same.

Me: But they are different. Last year, in 2017, the S&P 500 index return was 12%, and the Dow Jones Industrial Average was 14%. So if my return is 13%, did I beat it or not?

Him: Well, you pick one.

Me: You're telling me to beat the market, it's your challenge. I'm asking you to define my benchmark. I don't want to be accused of cherry-picking or moving the goalpost.

Him: Well, let's use Dow.

Me: Okay, well, good. They are two different indices —number of stocks, historical returns – even how they are calculated. *Do you know how the Dow Jones index is calculated?*

Him: Uh, sure, you take the number of shares - multiplied by the price.

Me: No, that's for the S&P 500 Index. You chose the Dow Jones Industrial Average. The number of shares of the companies is not directly part of the calculation for the Dow Jones index return.

Me: By the way- it's the stock price by a constant divisor for the Dow Jones Index, which determines the way you calculate the return, and by "beating," *what length of time are you using?*

Him*: I don't know, a year.*

Me: *How many periods are we measuring? Monthly? Quarterly? Weekly? Daily?*

Him: We'll measure monthly.

Me: Okay, 12 data points. By the way, that's the least amount of data points to determine a risk measurement, which we'll get into later.

He started to see I'm getting serious about it. I think the kids say "you don't want that smoke" – from a financial perspective.

Me: Okay, so 12 data points determine if I beat the market, okay, good. *Now, is it the number of wins, or is it by overall percentage?*

Him: I guess the percentage. Does it matter?

Me: Well, I want to be clear since the number of wins is like a batting average. My portfolio outperformed the stock market 7 out of 12 months, and then there are the raw overall percentages, 8% vs. 6%.

Him: I want the overall percentages because that's what matters.

Me: "Okay, alright, because you do realize the downside is your investment may be losing or underperforming until November or December, like one famous portfolio manager in 2008, and then crush it the final month. But you've got to stay with me. Will you hang in there?

Him: Yeah, yeah, I would. I made a bet.

Me: *What we SAY we will do and what we ACTUALLY don't always match-up.*

He chuckles.

Me: So let me get this straight. It's the Dow Jones, we'll measure it every month, and we measure it over a year, and we measure it by the percentage, and it's a raw return. Right? Okay, okay, good. So just so we're clear, this is just a raw return? *Are we using any other metric?*

Him: No, just return.

Me: Okay. So if I'm down 30% in the first 3-months - it doesn't matter.

Him: Well, obviously, I don't want to lose 30%.

Me: Oh, we're not talking about a bet, we're talking about your money here. This is your money. *I'm down 30%, you sticking with me?*

Him: No, you can't lose money like that.

Me: But you said that that's all it is, it's just the raw return. See, what we're dealing with here is, there's another factor called risk—no free lunch. The portfolio return turn negative, right? We need to look at the return and the risk. We can't just evaluate investment by their return – we need to evaluate them in relation to their risk factor. I could tell you I have a car that drives 500 miles on a tank of gas, but it would matter how big that tank of gas is, correct?

Him: Yes.

Me: Okay. Well, another analogy is that if I lived by the light rail, I could drive my car to work, or I could take the light rail. But if the target is to beat the light rail, a.k.a. the market, how do I do that? I drive faster? I run red lights? Did I cut people off? That's even more risk. Same thing, right? So to beat the market, I've got to do something decidedly different, or do something the same, but do it better.

Him: Correct.

Me: Yeah, okay. *So you're willing to take on more risk to beat the market?*

Him: Yes, okay.

Me: Okay, so we'll help you get that return. And yet there's a point where you say, that's not acceptable, right? Okay, just want to make sure we're on the same page. Okay, so Dow Jones, one year, 12 data points, overall raw return, don't care about risk unless it's a catastrophic risk. *Is that what I'm hearing?*

Him: Yeah.

Me: Hmm, so let's just say the market returns zero, and I return 2%, but you've outlined your retirement goals, and to retire - you need 5%. I beat the market, do you win?

Him: Well, no.

Me: But I beat the market.

Him: Yeah but…" (as his mouth starts to say, "That's not the whole story…)_

Me: Okay, so let me outline another situation. Again, more risk, more return. *Let's say the market returns +10%, and I give you +20% at the end of the year, but sometime during the year, I return +20%, my portfolio loses half of the value -50%. Is that something you're okay with?* And by the way, this is the money you need to retire on.

Him: Lose half of my money?

Me: Well, you know, that's what happens, right? When you try to beat the market, you will have periods when the return is negative, and to beat the market, sometimes you have to double down, right? If that's the only goal. The other one is, let's say the market is negative the whole year……sometimes we forget the market does have negative annual returns, right? 2008, the market returned -36%, and I'm down, let's call it -25%. Are you okay? You asked me to beat the market.

Him: No, well, that's still not good. But, you know...

Me: I won, and you lost. Literally. Your "beating the market" goal may not align with your need to achieve your financial goals.

Him: Well, yeah.

Me: And, in fact, the advisors' value may be more than the selection of the investment. Maybe it's an after-tax decision, or taxable decision, or something that reduces your risk in a specific asset class, or it's protecting your portfolio from loss of purchasing power. Those are all part of it, too, right? Let me just ask what if you come to me, and you really don't have clear goals? Or you have goals, but they're not really measurable, attainable, and dare I say…….*realistic.*   But I help you define and align those goals. Is there a value to that?

Him: Yes.

Me: But that has nothing to do with investments.

Him: "Yeah."

(And I kind of let him off the hook.)

Me: Look, I understand. You were raised in a world where people expect your investments to beat the market. I get it, I really do. Make no mistake about it, that's an institutional model, and those institutions are meant to last a long, long time—many beyond a lifetime. And sometimes, in perpetuity, when you talk about foundations, and endowments, and trusts. But in your case, if you have a finite risk tolerance and a finite time horizon, and if your returns may have some irregularities, such as you really don't want large negative returns, even when they "beat the market." And even positive returns that outperform on a percentage basis may not meet your goals based on other factors like taxes, inflation, even liquidity. You might not want to focus on just beating the market.

Me: So, in that case, maybe asking someone to beat the market isn't the right question

Investment Vehicles

Previously we highlighted the concepts of risk, return, and putting multiple investments together. A common question to investment professionals, "Is X stock a good buy, or what should I be buying?" I rarely give investment advice about individual stocks or companies—especially on social media. But I want to make some educational points when evaluating any "new" kind of investment.

The first point is that you want to clarify whether you're talking about "investing" or "trading." Trading refers to buying and selling for short-term results—let's say less than a year—and investing in the longer term, ideally more than a year. There are a lot of useful resources out there if you want to look at the differences between the two. But regarding investing, you want to understand the value of the investment now and the expected value in the future. The difference between the two will produce the expected return. What is the value now, and what will it be in the future? And you want to have a very clear timeframe on making that decision. You need a timeframe; otherwise, you run into what I call the Vegas effect.

Do you ever talk to someone coming back from Vegas? If you ask, "How did you do?" they usually tell you how much they "won," but depending on the person, they usually give the amount they were up (high point) first, then what they came home with or the use of the funds during the trip. If the timeframe or exit point isn't defined, anyone can tell you how much they made but is that over one month or one year? Did they sell it (a.k.a. leave the table?), or did they leave it on the table to let Vegas do what Vegas does?

The second thing to look at is the risk profile, which refers to the unexpected consequences of the investment you're evaluating. **Remember, there's no such thing as a free lunch**. Look at the return on the investment (ROI), and not taking the risk into consideration is where people get into trouble.

The third thing—often overlooked by investors and investment professionals—is that typically you're not buying investments in isolation, whether it's bitcoin, or stocks, or your house. You want to understand how each investment fits in with your other investments and understand how the price(s) move together.

There are plenty of books on investing, and I don't pretend to know the secret to make you rich in the stock market in the short run. Since the market historically has positive returns roughly 70% of the time, I would equate the ability to make money with financial assets over some time to a decent blackjack player that can win enough to cover expenses while living in Las Vegas. Sometimes you win, sometimes you lose, but over time you do alright.

Stock Market Movements

An ocean shore can illustrate how to think about the stock market. Every minute the tide will come in at different levels. If you put a mark in the sand and measure it every minute, you will see that sometimes the tide goes beyond the line, and sometimes it's a bit short. Most people ignore the actual wave coming in on an individual basis unless they're building a sandcastle. The tide rolls in and out daily.

Think of that as the yearly returns. Most of the time, we feel confident on the high low points based on the lunar system.

Historically, most of the time, the stock market is up. But sometimes we have storms. If you live in Florida, Louisiana, or Texas, you can't predict storms, but you know the weather can be disastrous any given day.

View the market as such. Even though the stock market has averaged about 9% over the last 20 years, it has never actually returned that number. The average is just that: an average. Sometimes external events will cause it to go high. Tide out – "Oh, look all the clams that we can harvest," or tide in – "A storm, a bad market, and the house we built on the waterfront are in jeopardy." By nature, that is the market. Predictable like an ocean tide.

Revisiting Investing vs. Investment and Saving vs. Savings

Sometimes we hear the words "investment" and "saving" as verbs, confusing them with nouns. Your company pays you to do a job: that is effectively your income. You two can choose to spend that money in the current period. We will address joint versus separate accounts later. Anything you don't spend is considered savings, as in the act of not spending. That act can result in money in a retirement account, savings account, or even a checking account when you don't spend the money in the checking account in the current period.

Savings, the noun refers to the amount that is set aside. You can not have savings unless you save. The noun **investments** only comes from the verb investing. In other words, you can't grow what is never set aside from spending. The same thing can be applied to the noun savings – which only comes from the verb saving or not spending. Savings are generally used for unexpected expenses –think rainy day fund. *Investments* can be thought of as *savings* with potentially more growth potential.

On the subject of banks, Traditionally, checking accounts paid little or no interest. And that makes sense: a bank isn't going to pay a lot for the money that may or may not be around in the short term. Savings accounts used to pay a little more to incentivize people and businesses to keep it there. Now, savings and checking are so close in interest rates they are almost indistinguishable, outside of incurring a small penalty for posting too many transactions in savings accounts within a period. That's the bank's way of saying, "Hey, you said you were going to keep a certain amount here, and there's too much activity." They need consistency to lend against those assets. Some may not like big banks or banks in general, but without banks, you'd pay for your house in full; businesses wouldn't have working capital, and you'd have considerably fewer options for investing. Most of us need banks.

Revisit – The Stock Market Is Not a Given

Here's an analogy. Go to any playground with kids. Wait for a parent to tell their kid it's time to go. Observe if the kid complies. Smart parents give a countdown and offer choices. The rookies (or those set in their rookie ways) just announce, "It's time to go," with negative consequences for noncompliance. The likelihood that the kid will follow directions is the likelihood that the stock market will go as planned or better. Some will comply, but there's always a chance that they will do their own thing. Returns from the stock market are not a given, and there is always a random component. Stocks can and do go down. That is not anyone's fault because the stock market is just a combination of future expectations on a basket of stocks. Historically, the stock market return is positive; about 70% of the time and negative 30%. But like our relatives who tell great stories with 70% accuracy, it's the other 30% that causes the real challenge.

Insurance: It's Not About You

While we're talking about risk in *Marriage & Money*, we should address insurance. You should have auto insurance if you drive, homeowner's/renter's insurance, and other property/casualty policies that make sense for your situation. But what about life insurance? This decision confuses a lot of people.

I do NOT sell insurance, and I never have. I'm not paid by any insurance company, agent, or broker, but I've definitely incorporated insurance into financial plans. The reality is that when you're on your own, living by yourself, you typically don't think about life insurance because you probably don't have anyone depending on you or your income. For the average single person, protecting other people after you're dead isn't usually a priority.

But now that you have a new, permanent dance partner, you want to think about how you can plan for when either one of you steps off the dance floor. Here's the key: Insurance is not about either of you individually. It's about safety and protection for the other person. If and when you have children, life insurance becomes even more important.

One important note: I'm talking about *term* insurance. The goal is to replace potential lost income. In its simplest form, that means that you pay premiums (usually annually) over a period of time, say twenty years. If you die within that time frame, your named beneficiary receives a pre-determined amount of money, tax-free, assuming the terms and conditions of the policy are met.

Before you ask, "What are the chances of me or my partner dying or becoming disabled at this age?" remember to **expect the**

certainty of uncertainty. The statistics regarding long-term care are included in the Do-What-You-Want section. While counting on your kids to take care of you in your final days might be tempting, you may want to have a contingency plan. Pure long-term care insurance can be hard to find and expensive, so a hybrid option of life and long-term-care insurance is one option to consider.

There are other types of policies that treat life insurance as an investment. They use similar underlying investment vehicles like equity, fixed income, and cash to create the value (cash value) for you, the policyholder. Products vary by duration of the contract, payment amounts needed, frequency of payment, beneficiary (who receives the money), ability to withdraw funds, etc. As you can see, they can be complicated. It's ~~important,~~ essential that if you work with someone – they completely understand these products. When you consider life insurance, especially as an investment, also consider whether the person selling insurance to you understands your full financial picture. If the insured person doesn't ask/care about the partnership's overall needs, the policy may not match your needs.

Annuities: Converting a single amount into a steam of income

In the "DWYW" section – we identified the challenge of taking a lump sum and converting that into a stream of income payments for expenses each year for an uncertain number of years. Think of the payout options for the lottery. Remember: the life span is the period ending with the last surviving partner. The accumulation period is the time to building wealth for future use. It's the primary focus for those working until they stop working. However, making that lump sum last is another challenge called the decumulation period. How much should a partnership spend

each period, let's say annually if they have a fixed lump amount –
let's say five hundred thousand or one million dollars?

Annuities are a vehicle that provides a level of certainty. By paying
a lump sum or fixed amount for an annuity – the annuity company
will pay a stream of payments for the rest of your life, possibly
even your surviving partner. You can pay one amount in the
beginning, or make a series of payments over a period of time.
You can receive the income stream immediately or some time out
the future. You can choose to receive your payment at the
beginning or end of a period. You can lock in a period that pays
you or the beneficiary for a defined period – for example, 10-20
years or for one person's lifetime or for the person who lives the
longest.

The good news: you have a lot of options. The bad news: you have
a lot of options. Related to costs: there is no free lunch. So the
annuity price includes the cost of removing the risk of the stock
market decline and you outliving your lump sum, depending on
the type of annuity selected. Once again, highly recommend
consulting with a professional.

Mutual Funds / ETFs

Mutual funds are a basket of investments designed to meet a
specific goal. Instead of individuals picking their own individual
investments and trading them based on market conditions,
mutual funds create an **investment bus**. You can jump on the bus,
and they will take you where the bus is going. Some are designed
primarily to preserve capital, which means they focus on "not
losing money" and offer limited growth. Others are designed for
more aggressive growth.

One of the risks of investing is the chance that a single investment
can result in significant losses or even result in the investment
being worth nothing. By investing in a basket of investments, you

reduce that chance. You don't own the actual investment inside the mutual fund; you own a piece of the mutual funds and everything that comes with it.

The downside is that you can't walk up to the bus driver and tell them you don't like certain people riding the bus; you can't personalize the portfolio's investment. Generally speaking, you can't tell the bus where to stop: All purchases and sales happen at the end of the trading day.

Want a different experience? Exchange-traded funds or ETFs offer the rideshare experience, like Uber or Lyft. You still don't own or control the investments, but you have more control over when to get off – intraday trading. There are some tax benefits of an ETF versus mutual funds.

Buying your investment individually is like buying your own car. If you choose to use a professional – you have your own driver.

To carry out this example – insurance and annuities as an investment is more like a train. It has limited stops but is efficient with getting you to a pre-determined destination.

One word of caution – some people place a large focus on the cost of the vehicle. Cost does matter if, and I really want to stress IF, everything is equal. **Whether evaluating a phone, a house, or an investment, you want to fully understand what is received in product AND service compared to the cost**.

What is the best investment?

This is a typical question: What is the best investment? Of course, any answer that doesn't incorporate time horizon, risk tolerance, or other preference is dangerous for both the person providing the information and the person receiving it. Putting that aside, let me offer a perspective.

What if I walk up to you and ask, "What is the best car? What is the best neighborhood? What is the best college? What type of snowboard should I use?" You can reply based on your own experience and decisions, but most people would recognize the question's disconnect without knowing more about my preferences.

Asking a financial advisor—who takes a variety of inputs to develop a recommendation—what a person should do, out of the blue or without additional information, is the equivalent of asking a really good chess player -who happens to pass by you two playing -*what should we do next*. Any reasonable chess player takes in previous moves and future moves. In other words, what could be a great next move is only as good as the ability to execute on the strategy going forward – generally speaking.

The more appropriate question may be: What opportunities or undervalued investments do you see in the market? When good investment professionals hear one-size-fits-all solutions for every client, we cringe.

Small Business

Owning a business can be very advantageous from the standpoint of personal enjoyment and financial benefit but make no mistake about it: it involves knowledge, capital, and work. There are two financial values of a business: the cash flow that the business generates AND the value of selling the business. Regarding your value to the business, your involvement could fall into three categories. This was pulled out of the book *The E-Myth Revisited: Why Most Small Businesses Don't Work and What to Do About It* by Michael E. Gerber.

    1)   the value of the technician, someone who works in the business;

2) the value of the management; and
3) the value of the owner and the entrepreneur.

If you ever thought about starting your own business or making your side-hustle a more significant part of your income, this book is a good start.

And the same could be true of a partnership. The reality is that some of us are really good at some of the day-to-day minutia (technical stuff). Some of us are really good at managing who does what or allocation of resources (manager). The other part of us might be really good at looking forward and how things will progress (entrepreneur). To be clear, related to your partnership, all of those parts or different roles are valuable, and each person inside the partnership brings their skillsets. The challenge is to identify who can do what – and seek outside help when needed.

Business Succession

One of the key reasons I started Marriage & Money LLC is that some business owners I worked with were baby boomers in a partnership. As they approach their DWYW period, we would discuss how they were going to monetize their business. In other words, how were they going to sell their existing business (as an on-going concern) for a price. A simple subtraction of liabilities from assets leaves the company's tangible value, but as we discussed in "Off the Books," there is more than just what's on the income statement (cash flow) and balance sheet.

Some of you will inherit a family business or take an ownership role in a company. There are many, many business owners that would love to work in conjunction with their successor as an employee and eventually have them take over their business. And not only from the standpoint of keeping the business going because they believe in it, but also from a monetary standpoint, where the owner can obtain the business's value -beyond the value of net assets and net cash flow.

Here's the rub. Many business brokers work with businesses close to the actual transaction sale date - let's say less than six months from the close of the company's sale. If you own a business, there's a lot of value setting up the business to prepare for the transition more than six months out. It may take two to three years to identify the successor, set up the operations, and identify the areas for improvement that probably won't be improved by the current business owner. It takes time to work out the details of how the business transition will take place and the way that the value will transition to the new owner. You can consider this type of arrangement to monetize the selling of the business to fund your retirement.

This is not true of all businesses. Many businesses are based on what the owner contributes. The value of the business considers the value of the owner's contribution because, in the absence of that owner, someone else will have to be paid to do that work.

The value of a good hairstylist is primarily with the people who work there. If Christy owns and works inside a hairstyle business but later sells the business and no longer works at the same business, how many current clients will stay with the new owner? This is a challenging but relevant question to address when selling a business.

I've worked with plenty of businesses where the business owner has not identified how they will transition. That is an opportunity for a potential buyer to consider versus someone starting a new business from scratch.

Running a Business

Over the last decade, I've worked with business owners as clients, served as a board member and loan officer for lending institutions, taught an Small Business Association (SBA) financial statements class, presented personal finance classes to graduating college seniors, and generally observed best business practices. I'll highlight four things that are obstacles for businesses to grow and survive.

These areas typically separate side hustles from legit businesses—*legit* meaning that you can count on this income and plan to grow it for future purposes.

1.   **Operational** requirements such as registering as a business with the city, county, and state are appropriate for your location. Paying the appropriate licenses and fees ultimately means paying taxes. Setting up a calendar and reminders can keep your business running smoothly.

2.   **Marketing.** As an owner/operator, likely, you wear several hats including sales. But marketing is the game plan to attract more appropriate clients or sales. Marketing is not just about flyers if you're a real estate agent or a neon sign for a restaurant or barbershop. Referrals are great, but to count on referrals without additional help could prove challenging.

How do you increase your (sales) revenue within the framework of your business? Here is the classic tradeoff: Should you take time to learn to post to social media or outsource that task? Even if you know how to do it, the E of TEAM—energy or effort—comes into play. Marketing can be as broad and complex as finance, so understand your needs, and if the services produce the results, you want in aggregate. It's essential to connect the dots and beware of the "all you need is..."

Here's a comprehensive list of the elements of internet marketing from Mainline Media LLC that cover the elements of marketing.

| | Marketing | Website | |
Development	Design	Social Media	Directory Listing
CMS	Photography	Blogging	Lead Generation
Motion	Illustrations	Social Networking	Paid Listings
E-Commerce	Images	Shared Media	Rating & Review
Rich Media Responsive	Fonts/Layout Colors/Patterns	Bookmarking	Free Listings
Strategy	Branding	Advertising	Public Relations
Attract	Position	Affiliates	Articles
Engage	Message	Blogs	Press Release
Inform	Relevance	Ad Networks	White Papers
Convert	Clarity		
Email Marketing	Content	Research	Traditional Marketing
List Building	Benefits	Audience	Events
Landing Pages	Credibility	Competition	Print
Design	Call to Action	Situation	Mass Media
	Search Engine Marketing		
Deploy		Pay Per Click	SEO

Source: MAINLINE MEDIA, LLC

The Internet Marketing Tree Version 2.1

Questions:

- What elements do you have and what is needed?
- What is missing from your plan?
- What can your marketing specialist provide and how well will the services integrate with the other components of your plan?

3.   **Bookkeeping.** There are many costs associated with running a business beyond reporting taxes. Financial statements are critical to understanding and managing your business. Expense items differ depending on the type of business: a brick-and-mortar storefront, online business, or service. Most people understand their direct costs—material and labor—but may miscalculate the standard indirect costs such as rent, utilities, cleaning services, transportation to pick up material, cellphone service, and internet service. Back to understanding <u>What You Have Section</u>: these expenses one time or reoccurring, fixed versus variable, and where do they fall on the hierarchy of needs for your business.

All are essential (or near essential) to run your business, but typically don't result directly in more sales. It's easy to fall into the trap of thinking, "If my internet speed were a little faster, I would increase my business X%."

The store furniture was a little nicer
The store lighting was a little brighter
The store sign could use an update.

If you take out a loan, the lending institution may provide resources regarding help in these areas. Just like finance, it's critical to see the big picture. Similar to marketing, should you take the time to learn bookkeeping software or outsource it? Think TEAM resources.

4.   What is your **expected or planned growth**? According to an old business saying, "if you're not growing, you're dying." It helps to have a growth plan at the risk of sounding morbid—even when you don't control all the inputs. Once you have a grasp of your business, understand how much TEAM is needed, including resources paying for your labor in the business. This means that if you work in the business, your time is worth a certain amount.

Starting out, people will allocate resources for fixed and variable expenses and direct and indirect expenses. Anything left over is paid to the owner. Ultimately, some people find that they are working for a dollar amount that's not appropriate considering the time, energy, and ability. As a self-employed business owner, do you know roughly what you are paying yourself? How much time will it take to wear all the hats in your business?

There are many more aspects to successfully running a business, but these four are prevalent obstacles for business owners with few or no employees.

Is this entirely different than running your "partnership business" with your partner?

Don't Call Me a Financial Planner

I wish I could put this into the fiction section, but outside of the reunion event, this is from a combination of conversations I've had with my good friend Charleston.

It's Friday at 4:30 pm, and I'm wrapping up work and my friend Charleston calls.

Roderick: *Hey Chuck. What's going on?*

Charleston: *Just checking in with you. What're you up to?*

Roderick: *Oh, just wrapping up the week.*

Charleston: *You still selling that slow growth fund? I want half of that when it goes on sale.*

Roderick: *There's no such thing as a slow growth mutual fund, and THAT is not how buying mutual funds work.*

Charleston: *Riiiiiiiight. Anyways, a bunch of us are going down to Jude's in Rainier Beach. -Want to join us?*

Roderick: *Man, I'd love to, I'd really love to. But actually, I have my 25th college reunion this evening.*

Charleston: *25 years? Time goes by fast.*

Roderick: *You know it. I'm actually pretty excited about it. I mean, it's been a while since I've seen those old classmates and teammates. Wonder how Lowe and Mattioli are*

> *doing? Maybe I'll impress my old girlfriend. Bought new clothes, been working out, haircut.......and you know the best part? Once they hear I'm a financial planner, boom! Game over.*

Charleston: *......Yeah, about that ...*

Roderick: *What? Is it about the haircut? I asked for a #2...*

Charleston: *Don't tell them you're a financial planner.*

Roderick: *Wait, what you talkin' about, Willis?*

Charleston: *Man, you know I love you, right? Well, here's the deal. Financial planners are to the finance world what dentists are to the medical community.*

Roderick: *I don't get it...*

Charleston: *I mean, look, it's not like you're an investment banker or some venture capitalist. You're telling people stuff that they should probably already know. And even when you're right, the results don't show until years later. You're talking about stuff way out in the future. At least with a dentist, I get a swag bag. Do you have any swag?*

Roderick: (Looks down at his desk)   *I have a "Growth of $100" chart but not really.... but if I'm not a financial planner, what do I say?*

Charleston: *I dunno. Tell them you're a model.*

Roderick: *A model?* (smiles)

Charleston: *Well, I meant more like a hand model.*

Roderick: *Oh ...* (smile drops)

Charleston: *Realistically, more like a teen hand model.*

Roderick: *Okay, that's enough.*

Charleston: *Sorry, man. And about your clothes for the reunion...*

Roderick: *Is there a problem?*

Charleston: *It's not-a-problem-Per-Se... but, well, for example, your pants...*

Roderick: *What's wrong with my pants?*

Charleston: *I know you wear extra mediums, but there's fitted, and then there's maybe TOO fitted.*

Roderick: *You think?*

Charleston: *Well, last time we were out, we could count the change in your pocket.*

Roderick: *C'mon, CG.*

Charleston: *It was two quarters, a dime, and three pennies. And the quarters were from 1994 and 2003.*

Roderick: *That's not good.*

Charleston: *Nope. Annnd ... your shirt.*

Roderick: *I'm wearing a white dress shirt. Can't go wrong there.*

Charleston: *Does it have short sleeves?*

Roderick: *Well, yeah.*

Charleston: *Is Mississippi still burning?*

Roderick: *Oh... (looking down) at least I have a nice jacket to wear over my shirt*

Charleston: *If you leave right now, you can return the jacket to your nephew's closet, and no one will know.   Look, I gotta run. Just relax and have a good time, okay?*

Roderick: *Sounds good.* Looks down at his shirt – *I prefer smedium.*

Choosing the Right Advisor

The financial picture within your partnership is a complex one. And it's not a picture so much as it is a movie—a journey. It's common to hire a guide for this journey. But how do you find the right guide? Many act on the recommendation of a friend or family member without asking the right questions.

Asking the right questions regarding financial advice is important. More than 250,000 people in the US that advertise themselves as "financial advisors." The goal of this section is to outline what to look for in a qualified advisor. As someone who has worked directly with and personally used a financial advisor for over 16 years and served as a financial advisor for my clients – I feel I can provide a unique perspective. But before I give you a checklist, I want to outline the evolution of financial advice as society's needs have changed over the years.

The Evolution of Financial Advice

Today, our financial needs are a lot different than those of previous generations. Let me give you an example - my parents moved to Washington state in 1973 after meeting at Grambling University. That year, my father started working at The Boeing Company, like many people in the Seattle area at the time. At that time, Boeing bore much of their employees' financial responsibility— just like many other large corporations. They offered an hourly wage or salary, possibly a bonus, and a benefits package that included health insurance, dental, vision, and life insurance. But most importantly, they also offered... a pension.

Generally, a pension is a promise to pay someone a dollar amount for the rest of their lives after they stop working, provided they meet certain requirements. And actually, it's not only for the employee's life but for the life of their spouse as the beneficiary. A company pension combined with Social Security alleviated a lot of the financial decision-making for the employee when it came to retirement. For the most part, the company did it for them.

Now, moving forward, this promise of a pension is feasible for ten, or a hundred, or even a thousand people. But when I interned at Boeing in 1997, the company employed 250 THOUSAND people. That's a BIG obligation for these companies, a significant liability. Starting in the 1980s, you started to see companies move away from pensions. This shifted the financial obligation away the company and back toward the employee.

Of course, that led to the popularity of the 401(k) plan—a defined contribution plan that both employees and employers can contribute to, rather than a defined set of pension benefits that the company promises to pay in retirement. Aside from employee matches, that some companies offer through the 401(k) plans, the responsibility to fund retirement was now largely on the employee. Retirement planning was pushed onto the employee.

This brings us to the evolution of financial advice as a service. If you think about financial advice, it used to come in the form of a stockbroker, right? They sold investments. People paid a commission and received the product. The advice was product-related, and any additional information was considered extra. Then in the 1980s and 1990s, as pensions shifted to 401(k)s, you started to see a shift from stockbroker to a financial advisor. Financial advisors provided advice on various investments—and they also shifted the compensation model from transactional (a.k.a. commission-based) to a fee based on a percentage of assets.

Ideally, the advisor's interests now align with the interests of the client. If the client loses money, the advisor makes less, and vice versa: When the client makes money, the account is worth more, and the advisor makes more.

I'm bringing this up because the advice moved from the "stock trade" to "investable assets." *But your conversations and decisions are more than investments. And the difference between a financial advisor and financial PLANNER reflects that fact—even though you might need advice on investments, the idea is to receive advice around all the other moving parts of your partnership finances, too.*

In 2020, financial planning is a big-picture assessment of your life. This picture includes things like understanding your goals, your cash flow, and your risk as individuals and together—not just your net worth. Investment management, stocks, bonds, mutual funds, even houses are just a portion of that. Financial planning also addresses taxes, inflation, retirement accounts, education goals, and even estate-planning concepts that consider the legal and regulatory environment.

As the needs of the individual have evolved, financial advisors are trying to catch up. And now, financial professionals like myself are trying to take the next step beyond what's on paper, and beyond the individual level. That's what *Marriage & Money* is: it's my attempt to help you understand you as an individual but also as part of this new partnership.

Most of the financial industry hasn't evolved to that point yet, and that's why this program is so important—and so different.

In my propinion: A large component of the right advisor or planner's value isn't special access to investment products or minimizing investments or trades' costs. The most valuable thing the financial advice field can do is help clients make better financial decisions through advice that incorporates and acknowledges the emotions that impact behaviors. It's a combination of traditional finance and the psychology of money.

The Financial Garage

When I give financial advice, I tend to make many analogies (in case you haven't already noticed). I like to use the idea of a home garage. The garage is your overall investment picture. And as we all know, some garages are well-organized; there are a place and purpose for everything. You can find everything easily.

And then other garages… Well, let's just say that for many households, the garage is simply a catch-all room. People store more and more stuff in there over a lifetime. In the case of your finances, you might store your old 401(k), company stock, savings bonds, and IRAs. Who knows what you might find in some of those boxes? If you're trying to understand your financial picture so you can create a game plan, you may need help organizing the garage.

You have to know what all is in the garage to use it effectively, right?

As a financial planner, the goal is to develop, implement, and monitor the strategy (the game plan), regardless of the particular financial "product."

Grouping Financial Advisors by Compensation Type

Because it's a broad field, let me distinguish advisors by compensation models. Each kind of advisor is useful, depending on your situation and your preferences.

1. **Commission.** This advisor sells stocks, bonds, mutual funds, insurance, or annuities, and they are paid for the transaction. This is the traditional stockbroker model. Outside of insurance, many in the financial services industry has moved away from this model—but it could still make sense when the client only needs access to a specific product and doesn't require service or advice going forward.

2. **Fee charged as a percentage of investment assets (AUM).** These advisors charge a fee typically 1% to 2% of investable assets. You might hear these advisors referred to as "wealth managers" because of their focus on wealth. Investments are typically stocks, bonds, mutual funds, annuities, insurance, and Exchanged Traded Funds (ETFs). An advantage of this popular model is the on-going relationship clients have with their advisors.

The Downside: the costs—an investable portfolio of $500,000 at a 1.5% management fee would cost the client $7,500 a year. Additionally, the advisor may focus heavily on the investable assets because that's how they get paid. The development and management of your full financial picture may be neglected. Also, there are account minimums for full service beyond investment trades.

3. **Flat fee/retainer.** In this model, the advisor is paid a set fee – unrelated to investable assets – to develop a comprehensive financial plan. Think of this as a business plan for individuals and families. The cost can vary significantly, depending on the complexity of the plan. It's essential to understand what services are provided with the fee, too. Downside: Usually, the fee only includes the development of the plan – flat fee. It's uncommon to include on-going work such as managing and monitoring investments unless through a retainer type model.

Fiduciaries: Acting in Your Best Interest

Have you ever heard the expression "fiduciary duty" and wondered what it means and who it applies to? In this segment, we will break down the fiduciary standard concept and explain why it could be a consideration in choosing your financial advisor.

In other words, a fiduciary duty is the advisor's commitment to put you as the client's interests first at all times.

What the Fiduciary Standard Is … and What It's Not
There are two standards of care in the financial services industry. The fiduciary standard requires advisors to always put their clients' interests first. The "suitability standard" requires advisors to make recommendations suitable to the client's financial situation.

The two are different and often confused. "Suitability" is typically determined with the questions you answer at the outset about your expectations for an investment's risk and return. The fiduciary level of responsibility is more complicated.

Think about the way you might treat a rental car — return it as you found it — is like the suitability standard. But the way you treat your *own* car? That's the fiduciary standard. Suppose you take a group of kids to the state fair, your responsibility as a child's parent – fiduciary standard. The responsibility of your kids by another adult is suitability.

There are more components to meeting the fiduciary standard, but here are some easy guidelines to follow when addressing a fiduciary related to investment advice.

> 1.   The advisor has a clear understanding of the client's financial situation and investment needs.
> 2.   The advisor needs to understand the investment they sell.

3.   The investment product's ability to meet the client's needs or make sense for the client. Furthermore, the advisor should connect the dots between client needs and investment products. Typically, the advisor needs to have a reason why this product was recommended or included.

4.   The evidence to support points 1 through 3 should be documented.

Before the big investment firms beat down my door to complain about my take on things, let me be completely clear: *Anyone giving financial advice can choose to do these four things and act as a fiduciary*.

I should also note that while registered investment advisors (or RIAs) are legally required to act as fiduciaries, and representatives of broker/dealers are not, this doesn't mean one is automatically better than the other. Representatives typically have access to more unique products than registered investment advisors, such as Initial Public Offerings (IPOs), special lending programs, etc.

But when you're evaluating either a service or some kind of investment product, there's always a risk/reward to consider. Suppose an advisor has satisfied the four parts of the fiduciary test. In that case, there's a higher likelihood they'll be able to provide you with a more detailed explanation of the pros AND the cons of your financial decision.

When you don't have that kind of relationship, and the advisor's interest is not necessarily aligned with yours, there's a higher likelihood that you're going to hear the pros of the product or action and less of the cons. It can be like asking a taxi driver the best way to go from the airport to downtown—will they tell you what's best for you, or what's best for *them*? Of course, ultimately, you're the one who's always responsible for your decisions. But a fiduciary is someone who should help you evaluate the various options in front of you. If you're at a fork in the road, they can tell you the actual risks of going left or right—and the potential rewards for each.

Experience

When you think about a financial advisor's level of experience, you want to focus on more than the number of years they have on the job. Their technical knowledge is essential, of course, but the # 1 attribute that people miss is the advisor's ability to evaluate risk.

Informed decisions involve both risk and return. Does the advisor's experience center around one strategy, with limited products? What is the range of investment solutions they offer or evaluate? What about market conditions? Good advisors acknowledge that we only control a portion of the variables that affect our plans and products.

Part of an advisor's responsibility is to assess how well any given investment or product fits *your* needs AND how it works with your other investments.

For example, you may have what we call a structured product, which is a product that's designed for specific needs. It has a certain return, and it has certain risk qualities. If an advisor is working with that specific investment, they're well aware of how it works independently. But, commonly, a client has just that one investment product. And the company or person selling the product may not inquire about all of those other investments you have.

It's your advisor's job to understand how that product fits into your total picture. That's why a good advisor provides value outside of access to investments. There's a technical aspect of understanding the investments that come with experience.

Experience means an advisor also understands the downside. When I started my career in 1998, the stock market was in a full technology swing. Then 2000-2001 happened; the tech bubble burst, and a bear market began. These radical shifts are prime examples of why you want diversification in general, but also why you want an advisor who understands the risks of market conditions and investments.

It's also important to find an advisor who knows how to communicate with you effectively and explain concepts you might not understand at first. Some of that comes through just knowing you and through your experience working together. But your advisor should generally be comfortable communicating complex topics in a way that you understand.

Now, keep in mind that advisors with more experience typically charge more by implementing account minimums. Of course, as with anything, that doesn't mean that the more expensive advisors are always better. But generally speaking, there's a relationship between ability and fees.

So how much experience **should** an advisor have? I think it depends on what you expect from them. Do you just want them to give you investment ideas? Do you want to collaborate with them? Do you want to just bounce your ideas off of them? Or do you want to offload all your responsibility and let the advisor manage your money for you? Your answer matters.

I'm not entirely discounting younger advisors. But there's no disputing that someone who has 30 years of investment experience probably has seen some things that an advisor of 3 years wouldn't have. It's challenging to find someone who has less than ten years of experience who has gone through both a bear market (stock market that has negative returns over an extended period) and a bull market.

Another understated value of experience is being able to help you manage your behavior— helping you to do the right thing versus merely telling you what to do, especially when it's not intuitive.

Here's an example: Remember the advice to "turn into the skid" when you hit a wet or icy patch on the road? It doesn't feel like what you should do at all, but it works. It's similar when the stock market declines—a lot of people are tempted to sell, even though they'll be getting a lower price than the day before. And buying doesn't *feel* like the right thing, even though it often can be. An experienced advisor provides behavioral advice critical to long-term success—because they've been there before.

Back to the ice: Until you hit an icy patch for the first time, do you really know what you'll do? It's all abstract until it actually happens—and when it does happen, it's nice to have someone around who can help you through the process.

That's why it's hard to automate financial planning, too. "Robo-advisors" or automated trading are popular today, and they will continue to improve. But the reality is that we're human. What we say we're going to do, and what we ACTUALLY do in times of stress and high emotion are two different things. **Robo-advisors and apps automate trading, but not your decision-making.** And they won't talk you down from the ledge when it's a bad day, and you're thinking, "I've got to get EVERYTHING out of the market." Or if stock market prospects sour, highlight alternative business or real estate ideas that might be more appropriate.

So how do you find an advisor with the experience you want? Just ask! They will tell you. Someone with fewer than three years of experience is a junior advisor—which is fine if that person is actively communicating with the rest of their team (which presumably includes more experienced members) and extending the benefit of the whole team's knowledge to you. But if the junior advisor is your sole source of advice, be cautious. And be aware—you might not save money by choosing a junior advisor. I haven't heard of many firms offering discounts for that.

With all that being said, you have to weigh an advisor's experience against everything else: their ability to communicate, their ability to navigate technology, and, quite simply, how you **feel** about them.

Choosing the Right Advisor: Collaboration

An advisor's ability to collaborate well with other professionals is relevant because all aspects of your financial life are interrelated. Buying a house has an impact on your retirement. Your retirement is affected by taxes and inflation. Your employment is your income source, which creates savings and investments that land on your partnership balance sheet. The insurance you need is dependent on your house and your life expectancy. They all typically have some sort of relationship with each other.

For some professions, collaboration comes naturally, such as real estate agents and mortgage brokers or wedding planners and event catering. Your advisor should be willing and able to collaborate with the other people involved in your financial life.

Let's say you're getting married, and each of you owns a home. How do you two decide your living situation, and how does that affect your finances? Do you want to sell the extra house or keep it and convert it into a rental property? What about keeping both properties and buying a third property to start new? There are a lot of financial and emotional components to what might seem like a fundamental housing decision.

Now think about all the professionals who potentially can be involved in those decisions: a real-estate agent, banker, insurance agent, tax specialist, legal advisor, and financial advisor. Each can provide help in their specific area, but typically they won't know or even proactively communicate with each other. If you have ever gone through the closing process on a home, you know exactly what I'm talking about.

And what about risk assessment? You need homeowner's insurance, but there are other risks to consider. If you hire a property manager, you've offloaded that risk, but if you're managing the property, you take on the responsibility and the risk, right?

Then there's the factor of asset appreciation (or depreciation). What does that look like over the period that you plan to rent out your property? Think about this from a banker's perspective. Let's say you decide to live in one house and rent the other house, but then you want to buy a third house—a bigger house that accommodates your new family. That factors into the overall financial ratios they will consider when determining things like your loan amount and rate. Now, what are the legal ramifications of renting your house? A lot of people don't think about this.

If you don't even know to ask these questions, you're probably going to receive limited advice. And when I say "limited," I mean that they're operating in the vein of their profession. It's not the real-estate agent's responsibility to tell you the tax ramifications of renting a property, nor is it their responsibility to explain the legal ramifications. But it's not instinctual for us to reach out to all these other professionals to see how each thing plays into the decision.

An advisor is someone who can sit in the middle and help you go through some of these more significant decisions—and know which questions to ask to help you make them.

You might think it doesn't matter, and you may be right—until it DOES matter.

License and Certification

Do you want a financial advisor who has a certification, or a license, or both? Well, first of all, let me start by explaining the difference between a certification and a license. A license means the state has granted the professional the right to offer you services based on minimum criteria. Why is that important? The answer varies by profession, but an industry license can offer a barrier of protection, akin to the concrete dividers on the freeway. They don't eliminate accidents altogether, but they significantly reduce them. In the world of financial advice, that's important.

Let's say your Uncle Dave has opinions on everything, and he has no problem sharing them with you. He might be right once in a while, but how often is his advice dated (best advice of the 20th century award has some dust) or not applicable to your partnership. That's why there's licensing for various professions, whether we're talking about your plumber, electrician, roofer, doctor, lawyer, or financial professional.

Certification is a different story. Certification can be useful to distinguish accomplishments at a higher level than licensing, especially when related to investment advice. But that is only if the certification actually MEANS something.

Certifications can help identify specific characteristics you might find desirable, though. Take, for example, the certification in financial planning—the certified financial planner designation, or CFP®. The right to use the CFP® letters or marks include demonstrating technical knowledge. Also, a requirement to have at least three years of relevant experience and pass an exam. You can't just start calling yourself "a certified financial planner"; you must meet the experience, exam requirement, and compliance record. Finally, there is an undergraduate degree requirement.

Which certification should you look for? It depends. If you want accounting, a CPA or Certified Public Accountant makes sense. If you want someone to analyze investments, a CFA® -Certified Financial Analyst may fit the bill. There are many more that serve specific niches. Typically, you want to look at the work experience and the technical requirements related to each certification. And most have some kind of regulatory, discipline, and ethics embedded, along with continuing education required to maintain the certification.

What's Right For You?

There's not one "right" financial advisor for everyone—because different people can have different situations, different needs, and different preferences. But if you ask the right questions and consider the right qualifications, you'll give yourself the best chance to find the right fit.

HIGHEST PRIORITIES

- Do you act as a fiduciary?
- How are you paid?
- Tell me about your training and experience in these areas, such as Goal Setting, Risk Management, Investment Management, Tax Planning, Retirement Planning, Education Planning, and Estate Planning.
- Are you able to show different scenarios based on changing variables?
- What is your work experience? What positions have you held?
- What did you learn from the experience of the market declines in early 2000, 2008, and early 2020?
- Do you have any certifications? How long have you had them?
- Do you provide perspective in areas outside of investment management? If so, what areas?

- How do you collaborate with other trusted advisors? CPA's, Insurance Agents, Lenders, Attorneys?
- Can you provide an example of a time when you collaborated with another trusted advisor outside your area of expertise?

DIFFERENTIATORS

- Do you offer opportunities for education, either live or on-demand? What are they?
- How can you save me time and effort in managing my financial picture?
- How do you handle clients who disagree with your recommendations?
- What additional services do you offer? Do you have training in these areas?

Behavior

I want to recognized behavioral performance experts, think2perform® for allowing us to use tenants of their Behavior Financial Advice® program for this section of the book.

Finally, where the rubber meets the road related to *Marriage and Money*: how our behavior— or what **we actually do** or don't do with our decisions—ultimately determines our success. Back to the restaurant example: you can have the best location, décor, staff, manager, even food, but all that can be nullified if your partnership decisions are less than desirable. Or, said differently, your choices need to align with your values and goals. So we will define behavior with regards to money: saving, investing, spending, and how it integrates with traditional finance. We will look at how emotions play a role and the neuroscience factors that impact behavior. And we will pull what we learned from the other segments to make better decisions.

In this section, we will:

- Introduce the concept of behavioral finance or our choices regarding money. What behavioral finance is and what it is not, and why it exists to understand WHY people make certain financial decisions/choices.
- Consider how our choices are related to our goals and values.
- Think about what we can do to make better choices.

Conversations and choices are mapped out with what we have, where we want to go, and how we will achieve our goals, with an eye on spending, savings, and investing. And traditional finance is about how to add or subtract investments based on risk, return, and how they move together, right? Not exactly.

We have to assume three things for traditional finance to truly work:

- People are rational.
- People are unbiased.
- People make decisions based on risk – how much they will lose versus the optimal amount of risk for the optimal amount of return.

Those assumptions are questionable—and that means traditional finance doesn't always work.

NEWS FLASH: People aren't always rational. They consistently have biases. And many won't take on the appropriate amount of risk due to being generally risk-averse. So while traditional finance is important, behavioral finance is, too—because irrational behaviors can lead to bad decisions.

Behavioral Finance

Behavioral finance is about how the mind and human behavior combine to impact finance—a blend of finance and psychology.

We often think of "the mind" and "the brain" as the same thing, but they are different. The brain is the physical structure that contains the mind. Think about the mind as the "musician" and the brain as the "instrument." We need both to function.

While our mind can reason, our brain has *chemical* responses to danger and opportunity. When something scares us, the brain innately wants to avoid it; when something excites us, the brain wants more of it. And the chemicals secreted in each instance ramp up one response while suppressing the other.

First, take fear. In a scary situation, your body produces cortisol (think of it as an alarm). And if you feel like you can't think straight, there's a very good reason for that: Cortisol reduces blood flow to our extremities which does affect our ability to think clearly because we're not getting enough blood flow to our prefrontal cortex. So, for example, you might feel fear about an event half a world away based on a news report—even if there's no solid reason for you to fear for your safety.

On the flip side, if your reward system is triggered, you get a shot of dopamine—that's more enjoyable, but it also restricts cognitive thought. That means I could be excited to proceed with something that might be risky, even though I cannot accurately assess the risk. (Think skydiving, investing in collectible Beanie Babies, or writing a book on *Money Conversations*.)

That's just what the brain does, though. Whether your company stock drops 20% in one day or an aggressive dog barks at you without a leash, both are scary. But they're also very different.

The trick is to try to get your *mind* to see the differences your brain can't, and then behave accordingly.

Otherwise, you can fall prey to "irrational exuberance" (a phrase former Federal Reserve Chairman Alan Greenspan used to describe the overvalued stock market in the 1990s), or "irrational anxiety" (fear that feels real even though in reality you're not actually in danger). You've heard of the term "*in your feelings*"; this refers to actions specifically driven by emotion.

Note that when I speak about "irrational" behavior, it is NOT gender-specific. It applies to everyone because everyone (excuse my absolute) can be, at times, irrational. I know some people pride themselves on being practical, rational, and non-emotional. You, my friend, are subject to bias and emotions, too—so don't look over at your partner. This is human nature. And don't think this is all fluff since this doesn't have to do with numbers, or that it doesn't apply to your financial situation, because it absolutely does.

But even when you understand your emotions, psychology, overconfidence, fears, and drive, you know what to do with that knowledge to make progress. This section is about how your partnership moves forward with this information. The integration of traditional finance, behavioral finance, and neuroscience ultimately sets the stage for better decision-making.

Behaviors, Values, and Goals

Your behaviors—or what you each do—affect your partnership. Essentially, they are the decisions you make. You want your behaviors to align with your goals and objectives, and you want your goals and objectives to align with your values and principles. Let's look at all of those.

Behavior is your thoughts, your emotions, and your actions. For our purposes, it ultimately means the financial decisions you make and the steps you take (both forward and backward) in your partnership—saving, spending, investing, etc.

Values are the most important things to you, the way you want to live your life, the way you believe things should be done. Of course, there's a challenge here: People often don't share the same values—even when they're in a partnership.

A quick side note: When some people hear words like "values," or maybe "principles" and "morals," they can get a little touchy. I'm not implying that your values are wrong if you don't have the same values as your partner.

Here's an example: What are your viewpoints on paying for your child's education? Depending on how you were raised or your own experience, your thoughts might be very different from your partner's. If both have the same beliefs or if one of you is indifferent – there generally isn't a conflict. However, sparks can fly when where values collide or conflict. The goal is to try to work inside the framework of what you already believe and understand, respect the other partner's position, and reach unified goals. Some might surprise you. It's not like we list our personal values for everyone to see on our LinkedIn profiles.

Goals—are yours just dreams, or are they actual objectives? (Hint: If you don't have them written down, and you don't have a plan, they're just dreams—whether you know it or not.) The best goals are SMART—Specific, Measurable, Attainable, Relative, and Time Sensitive.

Have you ever filled out a questionnaire asking for your financial goals? Were your goals SMART? Were they aligned with the values of your partnership? Were they aligned with your actual decision-making? Were they incorporated with your overall financial picture? If not, you can change that.

Why Behaviors Go Wrong

Our behaviors don't always align with our goals and values—sometimes, even when we know we're not doing the right thing, we just can't help ourselves. This isn't an excuse; it's just human nature. When you understand WHY this happens, you can take steps to correct it. Here are a few causes.

Part of the human condition we try to make things fairly discrete, binary, yes-or-no, easy. Experts say this helps us make decisions faster. Daniel Kahneman talks about it in his book *Thinking, Fast and Slow*. [Kahneman, D. (2011)] Heuristics is any approach to problem solving, learning, or discovery that employs a practical method but is not guaranteed to be optimal, perfect, logical, or rational. Instead it is merely sufficient for reaching an immediate goal. Heuristic methods can be used to speed up the process of finding a satisfactory solution. Examples include using a rule of thumb, making an educated guess, an intuitive judgment, a guesstimate, stereotyping, profiling, or common sense. Heuristics allow us to simplify problems, making it mentally as easy as sticking the key in the ignition to turn on the car.

Emotions. Remember how we said earlier that your brain is hardwired, with built-in systems that can produce active fear and pleasure responses? This impacts your decision-making and your partnership behavior. Have you ever been so mad—or so scared—that you couldn't think straight? That's not because you consciously decided to stop reasoning; the natural fight-or-flight response actually hampers your brain logic meter!

It's not just life-or-death situations that activate this response; frustration, anger, and other negative emotions can impact your ability to think logically.

Stress. In situations where we get stressed, we don't listen as well because we become cognitively impaired.

Allow me to unpack that statement.

When we are stressed, our listening, reading, and observation skills decline.

We are not in the best position to make reliable, rational decisions.

> **Questions:**
> - How good are you at recognizing your stress levels?
> - What activities do you engage in to reduce your stress levels?
> - What events, statements or people cause/trigger your stress?
> - Same questions for your partner. Are you able to recognize stress levels in your partner, beyond the obvious signs?
> - Can you safely inquire about your partner's stress?
> - Do you have tools to help your partner relieve stress?

Similar to the fight-or-flight scenario, when we're stressed out, we don't think as clearly (or as logically), and we tend to disconnect from other people. Maybe you close the door to "your" section of the house and just focus on individual tasks rather than bigger-picture goals.

That's a big deal because your partnership's success relies heavily on the relationship *between* the partners—that is, you. If you have trust and respect for one another (and treat each other accordingly), you'll be able to work together better, which means it will be easier to achieve your goals.

An essential step in your partnership's success is learning to recognize your stress and fight the urge to disconnect from your partner. Ask them for help, and give help when needed. Don't just say you have a partnership; ACT like a true partner.

Bias. It can be hard to admit our pre-judgment and biases. However, neuroscience tells us that we use these things to make quick decisions all the time. We all carry biases, and we pre-judge based on how we are hardwired. It's human nature. Here are a few of the biases we're up against when it comes to financial decision-making.

> **Excessive optimism.** We often look at the world through rose-colored glasses. Everything looks up: the economy, job, stock market, real estate. Your expectation is always positive, even though it may not be in line with more realistic views going forward.

> **Overconfidence.** This is optimism on steroids—it means incorrectly judging our ability to make good decisions. The irony is that this is often a product of success. For example, if someone flips a house and makes a nice profit, they may have overconfidence in their real estate ability. Or if they bought early into a stock like Microsoft or Amazon, they might believe they can pick winning companies going forward. It's hard to separate skill versus luck when evaluating your ability because you're not neutral.

> **Confirmation bias.** When you need to make a decision, who do you talk to? Typically, we seek people that agree with us; then, we accept this information as confirmation we're making the right decision. On the other hand, we ignore or reject those who disagree with us. One political party typically focuses on information from C** or M*N*C, while the other major party relies on F*x News. We know this, right? An alternative? What about seeking information from both or a 3rd source for a well-rounded viewpoint? Confirmation bias can be very risky because we won't get the unbiased input we need to make reliable decisions.

> **The illusion of control.** We believe we control things more than we do. Let's say you're in a car accident. You might think, "Wow, I wish I hadn't been going that fast," or "I wish I hadn't been on the cell phone just then." But the reality is sometimes the accident has nothing to do with what YOU did. We tend to have a false belief in our ability to control circumstances. You have to understand that

there are cases where your decisions simply don't matter—sometimes things are just out of your control.

Questions:

- Have you experienced any of these biases in the last month?
- Do you accept them or attempt to overcome them?
- What about your partner?
- Do you both feel comfortable letting each other know when one or more of these biases are present?
- Once identified, what are the next steps to overcome biases?

Money Disorders

Money Disorders are "persistent, often rigid, patterns of self-destructive financial behaviors that cause significant stress, anxiety, emotional distress, and impairment in major areas of one's life" (Klontz and Klontz, 2009)

<u>Types of Money Disorders include:</u>

Compulsive buying disorder (CBD) is characterized by excessive shopping cognitions and buying behavior that leads to distress or impairment.

Gambling disorder (problem Gambling) describes a **loss of control of gambling behavior** that causes significant problems with finances, work, or personal relationships.

Workaholism is working compulsively. A person who works at the cost of their sleep, personal care or connecting with friends or family.

Hoarding Disorder is a persistent difficulty discarding or parting with possessions because of a perceived need to save them.

Financial Denial is living beyond your means or in a way that your finances can't sustain. Typically justified by YOLO or You-Only-Live-Once.

Financial Enabling is when someone uses his or her money to try to keep another person financially needy and dependent for an indefinite period.

Financial Dependence is when one individual is financially responsible for another.

Financial Enmeshment occurs when parents involve their children in adult financial matters before the children are cognitively and emotionally ready to cope with the information.

Financial Infidelity is the act of spending money, possessing credit and credit cards, holding secret accounts or stashes of money, borrowing money, or otherwise incurring debt without the knowledge of one's spouse, partner, or significant other.

Money Disorders can derail the most promising partnership money conversation and decisions. If present, the next step is to seek qualified professional therapy where available.

Making Better Decisions

Law of Financial Planning:

The plan to have a financial plan will remain just that – a plan to have a plan...... until something "unplanned" happens.

When people hear this program is about making better decisions, they often feel I'm implying they *don't* make good decisions. "I already make good decisions," they say. But decision-making is best viewed on a spectrum. In your complicated life, you may make twenty complex decisions every month, in a mix of personal and professional situations – short, intermediate, and long-term.

And let's not forget, we make decisions that are self-serving and for the partnership. Now, let's assume out of those twenty, we make one great decision, five good ones, ten average decisions, and four that are "less than desirable."

```
 1 – great decision
 5 – good decisions
10 – average decisions
 4 – "less than desirable" decision
20   Total Decisions
```

What if you could move just one of those complex decisions every week from average to good? Or take a less-than-desirable decision, maybe one of inaction (which is a decision in and of itself), and move it to average simply by putting it on the to-do list?

Remember, this is at the partnership level. How many times do you not decide at all because there's a lack of communication, or emotions and biases that get in the way? On the other side, what about when you rush into a decision without the proper evaluation? Both of those can be just as challenging as the decision itself.

You *can* make better, more integrated decisions, and execute behaviors that overcome your partnership's emotions, communication hurdles. If you grew up in the '80s, you'd remember that **G.I. Joe told you, "Knowing is half the battle." N*ke has the other half handled with "Just do it." That combination usually equates to success.**

If you can move just one financial decision a week from less-than-desirable to average, average to good, or good to great, you'll be on your way to reaching your goals. For example, you might decide to leave your money where it is (proactive non-action) in the stock market even after the market dips—that's an instance where not doing something is still doing something. Or you two decide to plan a day getaway every six weeks to reduce stress, improve communication, and enjoy each other. Making better decisions should lead to better results – by having a process to make changes with regard to what you can control.

At this point, you may ask, "*Okay, what's a good decision?*" Well, we know it involves aligning the decision with SMART goals (both short- and long-term) and your actual values. We know it is technically sound based on technical principals of investment and understanding the impact on both cash flow and your net worth through your partnership balance sheet. Do good decisions ignore emotions? No, we understand how outside influences impact our emotions, so we recognize, reflect, and reframe though our logic meter, and then we communicate our thoughts. (think2Perform®)

Then we move forward with the best information available based on what we can control. It's not that simple to call a decision good/bad because your decisions are dependent on the situation. But if we understand what we can control and influence versus what we cannot control, we can feel confident that we made the best choice.

Control what you can control but account for everything you can measure

One important aspect is to recognize our level of control regarding future events. There are things we have total control over, other things we can't control at all, and then there's an area of "some control" between the two extremes.

Ideally, you want to leverage the things most under your control and carefully evaluate the factors that are somewhat or entirely out of your control. It feels pretty good to have some control over our future, doesn't it? Things like how much money you save versus how much you spend and what you spend your money on—these are completely within your control. What you choose to invest in and what percentage of your assets allocated to those investments—those are also totally under your control.

In the "Some Control" category, we have things like how much money you'll earn in your lifetime, and how long you'll live. Note, we cannot reasonably "make sure" that things happen as we like with things we don't completely control. The same applies to making guarantees.

"Out of Your Control" refers to things like what the stock market does; the return you'll see on some of those investments you chose; what other family members will or won't do; local and national governments tax and economic policies; and so forth. [GTR 2020]

And while it's easy to throw up your hands and say, *Well, I just won't even think about those things*, we can make plans that include these out-of-our-control factors and then adjust when necessary. It's the financial version of defensive driving.

Note that while you have total control over WHAT to invest, you have no control over HOW WELL the investment performs. Why is this important? People and partnerships may dismiss factors that are out of their control or make commitments they cannot keep due to events out of their control.

Let's Make a Budget (Revisited)

A statement that's probably been uttered thousands of times over the last month has been, "Honey, let's sit down and do a budget." It seems like a simple statement, and clearly, there's a group of people who jump in and execute. They may not do it perfectly or enjoy doing it, but they do it. And clearly, there is a group that just will **not** do it. But if you're thinking about sitting down and saying, "Hey, let's do a budget," it's probably not as easy as you think.

Somebody I have known very well for the last twenty years told me their partner made a career change. There was some angst about how it was going to affect their future. When I asked him, "How'd you address it?" he said he told his partner, "We should sit down and do a budget." And the reaction was less than favorable. When I asked if he had set a time and date for them to have the conversation, he said he hadn't.

I'd also pointed out that what his partner may have heard was, "You're spending too much money. I need to have better control of our decisions."

By now, you can see this guide is about much more than budgets. It's out in the future, but it's also a combination of two people and their needs and wants. While our basic needs may be very similar, our hierarchy of wants may differ based on our different values.

Before you get into the "what you should do" conversation, you may want to understand where your partner is coming from. That will help you understand the goals which will drive your decisions.

Instead of saying, "Let's sit down and do a budget," you may want to start backward and say, "Well, let's sit down and track what's coming in and what's coming out."

Try this: For the last twelve months, if you can account for eighty percent of where your money went, including taxes, then you're probably in the position to start a budget conversation. But suppose you can't account for eighty percent, seventy percent, or even sixty percent of where your money went. In that case, the idea of projecting now and being accountable may not be realistic.

One of the aspects we covered in the communication segment was understanding trigger words. Do you know your partner's trigger words? If you do, you may want to consider a more gradual way of getting into that conversation. Here are some ideas:

- Start the discussion with things you two enjoy.
- Talk about your dreams and things that bring you joy or happiness.
- Ask for permission to transition into financial decisions that impact the partnership.

From there, transition into a discussion about figuring out how to capture those experiences in the future.

Let's say a person enjoys going to the beach. If they're talking about the beach and how much they enjoy it, they might even say, "Oh, I'd love to go to the beach now." It might be the dead of winter. But now you manage the conversation as it relates to being able to go to the beach in the future and how you're going to execute that.

The conversation may not have a money overtone; you may just talk from a logistics standpoint first. But that still requires a combination of your resources and how to approach using them.

As you move along in your "money" conversation, linking your partner's enjoyment with how much money it's going to take might be a real turnoff. Instead, consider approaching the conversation from a broader perspective: How much **time,** how much **energy**, and potentially how much **money** will be necessary? Then, consider how that affects your intermediate and short-term goals. How do you integrate plans for meeting long-term goals? Have the budget conversation, but be aware of the inevitable hurdles. Pick a time and place when you're both in an open frame of mind.

Second, instead of starting with what you *should* do, maybe start with what you've done in the *past*. Create conversations about how you're going to get there with the resources you have. You can think of this as:

Doing what you Gotta, in order to do what you Wanna.

Back Burner

This is not designed to be a motivational book, but it's important to recognize the challenge: Money conversations are important but not urgent.

Steven Covey is noted for categorizing things related to: Urgency and Importance.
Urgent, Important - *We're on it!*
Not Urgent, Not Important - *Interesting, but we seldom get back to it.*
Urgent, Not Important - *draws our attention but may not be the best use of time.*
Not Urgent, Important - *Backburner.*

Money Conversations fall into the last group. Our challenge is to prioritize with respect to other things in our lives. I'll use a cooking analogy. Let's say we are using a BBQ grill outside –Grillin' Chillin' & Spillin' (knowledge)– while preparing other food. The cooking time will depend on the type of food, amount, along with other factors.

After putting the food on the grill, we may divert our attention to other things: checking social media, a conversation with our partner, or even paying attention to other food inside our home.

Typically, three things will bring us back to check on the food on the grill.

1. An internal clock that tells us to check on the food.
2. An external timer on our phone or someone telling us
3. We smell/see something burning.

We don't want to wait for "burning" regarding money conversations.

Better to "learn" than to "burn" in this example.

Do you have a day and time identified to address money conversations in your partnership?

Decision Model

Let's break down the decision-making process in a quick visual. When people have a money conversation or make a financial decision—whether it's short-term, mid-term, or long-term—they're by nature or out of habit, viewing it from an individual standpoint. Generally, we have four resources or factors to consider: Time (attention), Energy (or effort), Ability (Skill or Expertise), and of course, Money. Let's call it TEAM. Let's assume there is no free lunch, and generally, people are not in an altruistic mood.

If an individual has a decision to make, their main questions are, "How will this decision affect me? Is it going to make me function better in life? Will it give me a higher level of enjoyment?"

On an individual level, those questions are fine.

But in a partnership, you bring in another person, so you add communication to the analysis of any decision. The decision-making process is not just about saying "yes" or "no" to a choice. It's about determining whether the outcome of that choice will align with each of your values and goals. Making such an assessment can cause (who are we kidding - It absolutely does!) stress between partners, especially if you two have different value systems and goals. Each individual may be inclined to make different types of decisions.

This can be applied even before you say, "I do." As the partnership progresses to marriage, the parties look more deeply and say, "What are some of the things we're going to come away with after the wedding. It's a celebration. It's a chance for us to have a high level of enjoyment, incorporate our families, and get approval from our existing family."

And there are several parts there to consider. In general, we'll define short-term decisions as the time from the decision and results as less than a month. Intermediate-term decisions are those in which the outcome is expected from – thirty days to a year. People may engage professionals when making these mid-term decisions.

The challenge is looking at the long-term goals—looking out more than a year—such as buying a house, starting a family, advancing one's career, or retiring. Those decisions usually require one and often multiple professionals, and the outcome is dependent on several factors - several of which we may not control.

Many people engage professionals here, too, falling somewhere on the spectrum of "*I understand this*" to "*I get the basics*" to "*This is stuff I don't quite understand*" to "*I don't even know where to start*." And even people who work in finance may be in the category of, "Well, I somewhat get it." But at the end of the day, we want to have confidence the professionals we're working with understand what we are trying to achieve versus just going through the motions.

The goal is to outline how to incorporate the values of two individuals inside a relationship. That does not require every decision to be made equally or for both people to fully buy-in on everything. But aligning your goals with your values can help make effective decisions in the short-, mid-, and long- term.

Time

When you get married, there is an expect benefit of combined household finances. You now have economies of scale: two incomes and a combined household. Even if you've lived together previously, now you're truly combining your finances to receive the full benefit. Now, though, one of the things you have to manage better is your *time*.

For example, let's divide the day into twenty-four hours for a single person. If you start with the assumption of eight hours of work and eight hours of sleep, you'll have eight hours left for personal time. In reality, we make adjustments. Most of us don't work exactly eight hours every day. Some of us work more than eight hours when you factor in travel time to work, after-work activities, and our work-related mental engagement even when we're off the clock, the actual time spent committed to working is much greater than eight hours a day. Even if you're at home and you're *thinking* about work, your CPU is running.

When it comes to sleep, we allocate time, but the reality is that many of us don't receive enough sleep. After accounting for work and sleep, we're left with four to six hours of personal time.

Then what happens? We introduce a partner into the mix—the reason why you're spending time with your partner because you receive a benefit out of it. Remember, you can have a benefit for yourself and somebody else at the same time. Those two can be dependent or independent events.

When *you* do something, it's for *your* benefit. When you are *not* married, if you don't want to do something there is less of a commitment – generally speaking. When you *are* married, opting out is not as straight forward. It's a different game because now you're in a partnership, so you're making decisions for yourself *and* your partnership.

We decide how we allocate time, energy, and money based on what we receive as the benefit. Now you have to allocate time to your partner as well. The challenge is that you'll have to do things when you're not going to see the full benefit right away, but it will further the relationship.

There is an expectation—sometimes silent (non-verbal communication) and sometimes spoken— that the partners will spend time together. Now add children. You've already allocated your personal slice of time and your partnership slice of time, and now you need to trim those and allocate time for the kids.

What gets cut back? Unfortunately, a lot of us don't have the luxury of cutting back our work. Maybe you can cut back on sleep a little bit, but the reality is, whose time gets cut? Personal time.

How many of us have heard of parents going to the bathroom, closing the door, not to use the facility, but simply to shut the world out because they want to ensure they got their own time?

What we're really talking about is time management.

Try spending thirty minutes to scope out how your weeks and months look at a daily level.

How you can allocate resources, and leave room for variation when it comes to unexpected demands on your time? While this book is void of technology tips and hacks, how you leverage technology with regards to time is E-ssen-tial.

Are you able to communicate that with your partner and get all parties on board? There is a way to work within the confines of your resources that you can allocate to your kids, leave room for variation, and also allocate towards your spouse, all while having an understanding of the tradeoffs.

Finally, we acknowledge that values manifest in spending and how we spend our time. For example, let's use football as an example of how time and values are connected. Someone I knew before I was married (we'll call him Broderick Livens to protect his identity) would spend countless individual TEAM resources during the fall season watching games, researching, and discussing football. Not to mention the emotional impact he experienced depending on wins/losses. This value has its place in one stage of life but may pull Broderick's TEAM (time) resources from other important aspects of his life later when others are involved.

Chess vs. Checkers

Have you noticed other marriage and money programs are almost exclusively focused on a budget? Spend less than you make, and you win, they say. That's checkers. These days we are responsible for our transportation to the golden "Do-What-You-Want" chapter in life and other important partnership goals. Getting there is much like navigating a chessboard. You have a king and a queen, some other notable support pieces, and pawns in chess. Protecting the king and the queen is fairly obvious. Your rooks and knights and bishops are your other support specialists on the chessboard of life. How will you leverage them to their maximum potential? What is your strategy, so they work to support the king and queen, with minimal losses? Some people focus on the partnership conflict – one person versus the other, but, in reality, the partnership is successful when both people are working together versus against each other.

Believe and Verify

Do your research. A little fact-checking or source verification can go a long way. Choosing to verify doesn't mean you don't believe it. Fact-checking may be needed to build more confidence in your decision. Factor in the source. Generally speaking, nonacademic sources tend to have a built-in bias. Biases don't automatically invalidate information, but it can shape the narrative. Verification may take extra steps, but it yields a higher level of confidence in the decision-making process.

Putting It All Together

"I see" said the blind man as he picked up his hammer and saw.

Let's visit several real-life practical applications of addressing behaviors, emotions, and communication with your financial decisions. Let's put it all together with everything we've learned by walking through some examples.

Remember, the goal of *the Most Valuable Wedding Gift* isn't to make more money—it's about having better conversations, which leads to making better decisions. It's about acknowledging that you two are responsible for your own decisions, understanding and accepting the certainty of uncertainty, and realizing that you'll be more successful when connecting your values with your decisions as a partnership.

These examples are for educational, illustrative purposes only, and they shouldn't be taken as an individual or partnership-specific advice. And while I've talked a bit about evaluating investments, I'm not making specific recommendations.

Imagine you've just finished this program. You two think, "Wow, we've learned a lot, but there are a ton of moving parts here. How do we fit it all together?"

You should have a pretty good idea about how you want your partnership to operate. Let's begin with the essentials of sound financial planning: Evaluating what you have, where you want to go, and how you're going to get there.

First Thing's First: Have the Conversation

Engage each other in the all-important money conversation—whether it's to figure out your balance sheet, talk about your cash flow, or anything else—on a day and time when your energy level is sufficient. You can talk with each other without interruptions. Commit to these four things:

1. No phones or distractions.
2. Let your partner know in advance you'd like to talk, and how long you'd like to carve out time.
3. Give them time to respond and plan.
4. Ask for a mutual agreement of complete attention.

If one of you has to reschedule, that person should be responsible for finding an alternate day for the conversation. If you are looking for a catalyst, how about you put this on your calendar the next Thursday at 7:30 pm after both of you have read this book. If that doesn't work, look for the next mutual opening between Tuesday and Thursday between 6-8 pm.

What You Have

Review the section "What You Have" before proceeding. I will assume you have your joint cash flow and partnership balance sheet ready, and your values identified and aligned.

JOINT CASH FLOW

Some things to consider when it comes to cash flow:

1. The words "cash flow" can be intimidating. They can bring feelings of anxiety, fear, shame, or maybe just being overwhelmed or uneducated. So before you start digging

into the numbers, you may want to pause and consider how this phrase makes you feel. Does it make you feel excited? Anxious? Do you feel a little bit embarrassed? Are there any negative feelings? If your partner says, "Let's talk about our cash-flow situation," what's the first feeling that washes over you?

2. Do you understand the various factors that go into cash flow? Many people just think about income and basic expenses, but they neglect to factor in preventive care for their health, lifestyle choices, etc. These all affect our time, the money we make, and the amount we spend.

BLENDED BALANCE STATEMENT

The balance sheet for your partnership can also feel intimidating, and maybe even a little too personal—so you may want to start with something light, like what you two enjoy doing, then move on to generic goals and agree to write them down. Next, approach what you two have (assets and liabilities) to reach those dreams.

Remember – goals are dreams with S.M.A.R.T. details. Now that you're a partnership, you both will want know *everything* the partnership owns and owes. This is the first step toward creating a plan and a set of goals for the future.

As you're putting your cash flow and balance sheet together, don't neglect the discussion about values. It can be as simple as identifying five to ten values that you two share as a partnership and the most important values to each of you as individuals. It's critical to align your values with your goals.

Your values will shape the decisions you make. Writing those values down makes them more concrete. Post them somewhere you can see daily; this makes them stick. For extra credit, you can take pictures and create inspirational posters. Sounds goofy, but it works.

Lifestyle Creep

You've finally done it — you landed that new job. It probably took several rounds of interviews and a ton of studying and networking and countless online searches.

Who could blame you for wanting to reward yourself?

But it pays to be careful when you get that first new paycheck, especially if your salary has increased significantly — because this influx of money can start making things creepy.

Well, not *that* kind of creepy. (Unless this job pays you so much you have to start worrying about being kidnapped or something.)

No, we're talking about *lifestyle* creep. It happens when you walk into that gourmet grocery store, and all of a sudden, you can afford whatever you want — whether you need it or not. When you decide a new luxury car is in order, even though the sedan you have now runs perfectly fine. Or when you start thinking your apartment just isn't big enough, despite the fact that you have a room sitting empty right now.

A Natural Phenomenon

It's natural. You adjust your spending based on what you *can* spend, instead of what you *should* spend. Sometimes, the changes are small, like dining out more often or moving from generic juice to organic. Those things aren't going to get you into too much trouble.

But I have also seen this phenomenon, famously introduced by financial titan Michael Kitces of the *Nerd's Eye View*, at far more dangerous levels. Often, when one or more household members hit the "magic" $100,000 annual income threshold, they start thinking they deserve massages, club memberships, etc.

Their savings dollar amount may remain the same, even as the spending needle starts moving higher. Even worse, these folks are prime candidates for the Diderot Effect, which is the notion that buying new stuff can lead you into a spiral of buying even more new stuff. A new hat leads to new shoes. New shoes leads to new clothes. New clothes leads to……….

Of course, not all spending falls into the "frivolous" category — and the job of a financial planner isn't to tell you that you don't deserve that new car like some prominent financial personalities like to highlight, or that the generic cereal is really just as good as the brand-name. The art and science is to balance your decisions based on your needs, indirect needs and wants based on partnership income and future goals.

Where Do You Want to Go?

You know what you have, so where do you want to go? What are your hopes and dreams? This isn't limited to finances. Nobody really wants to have a million dollars just so they can look at a pile of money; they want that money because it *does* something for them, whether it's giving them the ability to travel, allowing them to quit their job, providing a feeling of security, or something else.

What do you two enjoy? What are your interests? Are they joint or individual?

GOALS – Retirement, Business Ownership, Children, Children's Education, Adult Education, Real Estate, Parent's Care, Community Work

It's time to talk about goals. Remember, goals should cover the short-term, intermediate, and long-term. The biggest overarching goal is typically retirement.

In theory, you make one goal (like retirement) your sole focus until you achieve it. But in practice, we juggle making progress toward multiple goals.

For example, you might want to move from working for somebody else to working for yourself. Or find a better job. Or the "standard" things like buying a house, starting a family, and providing for that family. Those goals are a little general, though. The best goals are S.M.A.R.T.: specific, measurable, attainable, relevant, and time-sensitive.

Here's an example of a goal:

"We want to be able to pay for our child's college education."

Let's turn that into a S.M.A.R.T. goal:

We want to save $10,000 a year over the next ten years.

That way, we will have $100,000 or more by the time our child is eighteen, and we can help them with the cost of college.

That goal is much better. It's Specific and Measurable ($10,000 a year). We'll assume it's Attainable with your partnership income level, and that it's Relevant in that you will or do have a child and they will want to attend college. It's also Time-Sensitive: a ten-year plan designed to help when the child is eighteen years old.

How to Get There

Knowing what you have is one thing; knowing what you want is another. But figuring out how to get there—and actually doing it—that's completely different.

If you're going to do it all yourself (with your partner), you'll need to create those S.M.A.R.T. goals we just talked about. And you'll need to factor in all of the variables and challenges, especially when it comes to retirement planning—taxes, inflation, longevity, healthcare, income, debt, and more.

It's a lot to deal with, which is why many people seek professional help. A good planner will do the following:

- **Have your partnership (not just one person) best interests in mind.** This is called the fiduciary standard, and it means that the recommendation they make, or action they take, is in line with what is best for you.

- **Get to know you.** It's hard to act in your best interest if an advisor doesn't connect with you to learn about your situation, values, and goals. Choose one that is genuinely interested in going beyond the numbers with you.

- **Communicate effectively, providing clear documentation and a written plan.** You should understand what the advisor is recommending and why. If you don't understand, keep asking until you do. A good advisor *wants* you to know what's going on.

- **Have the appropriate experience, certifications, and tools.** You're asking someone to help guide your financial life and provide advice to reach your goals. Ensure they're qualified to do it and have the right technology to help you. They also should have collaborative relationships with other professionals who might be necessary for your purposes, such as estate-planning attorneys, CPAs, etc.

- **Make you feel comfortable.** Do you trust this person? Do you think you'll like working with them? Do you feel they are addressing your specific situation, or are they just putting you into a cookie-cutter program? You want to feel confident about your choice.

Examples

Let's talk through some situations, numbers included, to illustrate how some of these *Marriage & Money* concepts apply. We'll look at two individuals who make $75,000 each; as a partnership, that means they now have a household income of $150,000. Let's say they want to retire in 30 years. What questions and situations might they face in the short-term, intermediate-term, and long-term?

In the Short Term: Building the Partnership

Our couple is married now—and for this exercise, we'll assume they didn't live together beforehand. So they have a lot of things to consider, including a few of the age-old questions:

- Should they combine their finances, or keep their own checking and savings accounts?
- If they keep their finances separate, how will they pay bills, taxes, and savings?
- Will one person be responsible for certain expenses, and the other partner responsible for a different set?
- If they combine, will one person manage the finances, or will those duties be shared?
- How will they manage budgeting and spending?

That's a lot to handle. And it starts with effective communication about values and habits. They need to have a detailed conversation (or, more likely, several conversations) to learn more about each other. Yes, they're married, and they've been together for a while, but as any married person will tell you, there's always something new you can learn about your partner. And you'd be surprised how many couples don't have a conversation about values—ever.

The couple starts talking about how each used to spend their own money when they were single, and why they spent it that way. They put together their cash flow and create a balance sheet for their partnership. Then they move to how they **want to** spend their money, now that they're together, and **why** they want a certain spending plan:

- What does each partner value?
- What spending and saving decisions will reflect those values?

After that, the choices around budgeting and other financial issues become more clear. As a bonus, by doing this, they're creating a pattern of good communication for other areas of their marriage, too.

The Intermediate-Term: Professional Changes, Buying a House

Things are going well. In fact, one person in our couple receives a promotion at work! Now they're bringing in $85,000 instead of $75,000, with the potential to make over $100,000 with bonuses. That's great news, but this partnership runs the risk of "lifestyle creep," or spending more because they're bringing in more. We see this a lot: a higher income means you upgrade your car, you're more likely to pick up the drink tab after work, upgrade your wardrobe, etc.

It's similar when two single people earning $75,000 each get married. Suddenly, they have $150,000 in income and roughly half the cost of living separately. It can feel like getting a big raise. I call that the "*lifestyle leap*" at the beginning of the marriage: double the earnings, half the spending.

In either scenario, no small decision alone will derail mid- and long-term goals, but when added together *they will have an impact*. Always evaluate financial decisions in terms of goals *and* values. What if the extra money from a raise went toward a down payment on a house versus leasing a better car? No problem, if that matches your values.

Let's look at another couple as an example. Before they bought that house, however, this couple did something very important, something that had nothing to do with location, or size, or even their budget. Regarding buying a house, they addressed the simple question: "Why?"

It turns out; they wanted to buy a house for one primary reason: for a place to raise a family eventually. Sure, they know that real estate can also serve as an investment, but they aren't counting on their home's value to appreciate at the current pace. Of course, it would be nice if it did, but it's only one piece of their financial plan, and they aren't relying on it to eventually fully fund their retirement. Again, it's something that aligns with their values.

In the Long Term: Planning for DWYW – Doing What You Want

So far, our couple is doing everything right. But after getting their financial house in order in terms of budgeting, and after buying their actual house, they find out they're *not* on pace to meet their retirement goals.

For this example, we're using the rough illustration of needing 75% of current income for a baseline of twenty-five years.

(You'll want to go through this analysis with more precision, and leave room for real-life events, both planned and unforeseen, but this will give you a template on how it could look).

Don't just plug any number here and call it good—whether you run it by a professional or create your own detailed plan. You *do not want to miss on this calculation.*

Sources of Income during Do What You Want Period

Understand that you're dealing with future cash flow every year, both in's and out's. Those ins include various sources of income: pension plan, 401(k), or another company-sponsored plan, IRA, social security, and passive income from stocks and bonds. It could include selling company stock or selling a business. It could include an insurance or annuity product. You may function as a consultant and earn in retirement. Even a primary residence or rental property can be a source of income in the future.

Why 75% of income? Some people might not think they'll need that much—after all, the house will be paid off, so no mortgage payment. But don't forget property taxes and homeowner's insurance, two things that many people don't think about because they're bundled into the mortgage payment they make every month. Your principal and interest each month are likely a lower percentage of your income than you think. *(According to the Bureau of Labor Statistics, housing costs for baby boomers are about 17% of income for renters and 19% for homeowners.)*

Also, even if your house is paid off when you retire, if you bought it thirty years ago, that means it's thirty years older, too. If you haven't remodeled, your kitchen and bathrooms are at least thirty years old. Other things are dated, too. You'll probably need a new roof, plumbing, and electrical work during retirement. You could have foundation issues. Are you going to do that all yourself? Maybe so, but there are materials' costs even if you do your own work.

Finally, the most frequently overlooked cost of all as you approach retirement is virtually invisible. It's called inflation. Inflation can kill even the most solid retirement plan. Why? Because people often fail to remember that everything will cost more in the future, and the buying power of a dollar today will not be anywhere near the buying power of a dollar in the coming years.

So we're going to stick with 75% of pre-income in retirement as our target. The good news is our couple knows this will work for them, at least given their current goals. They've discussed their values, and they know that while their expenses should be lower when they retire, they also want to travel extensively and ensure they have enough money for healthcare. They also realize that values can change over time, and they're committed to communicating regularly to check their progress and see where they both stand.

Continuing with this example, with a combined income of $160,000, how much do they need in retirement? 75% of $160,000 is $120,000. Our couple needs to create that much in real income for 25 years (and we need to adjust it for inflation over time). Why 25 years? There's a one in three probability the female will live to 90 or beyond, and roughly a 1 in 5 chance for the male. Even if one passes before that, there's nearly a 50/50 chance the surviving spouse will live to age 90 or later.

Adjusting for inflation, will they have enough replacement income to maintain their lifestyle over 25 years?" If they are not on track, that is not a show-stopper.

Remember, they have 30 years to make it up. They can adjust their investments, adjust their time horizon, spend less (b-word), attempt to make more within their current position, add a side hustle, or treat the in-laws better. Not tracking on pace for goals does not necessarily require making large adjustments all at once. It just has to average that over the 30 years.

They do need to address this deficit; otherwise, they might not be able to travel as much as they want in retirement. And just because they have a lot of time doesn't mean they can sit back and expect the stock market to go up, or their home value to skyrocket or assume they'll be able to get a higher-paying job down the road. Ask anyone who was around in 2008 how their financial situation felt then. The housing market crashed, jobs were hard to find, and the stock market certainly wasn't helping any.

Our couple may need to work with a professional to get back on track. If they have a plan, they may need to take a close look at why it's not working (or why they're not following it).

Our couple has a long time before retirement, so they might decide to increase the risk in their portfolio because taking on additional risk brings the potential of greater returns. But as retirement grows closer, the goal usually shifts more toward protecting what you have rather than seeking aggressive growth.

They may also need to take some basic steps, such as finding ways to earn more, spend less, or both. Maybe they fell victim to lifestyle creep, and they need to align their spending with their values better. When they get closer to retirement age, they might consider waiting to take Social Security in order to increase their payments, too.

Will Our Couple Make It???

There's no way to know for sure. Even though this scenario is fictional, we outline the principle of the certainty of uncertainty and identify variables that are within our control to increase our confidence level. The key for this couple and your partnership is to check in consistently along the way, so there's time to make adjustments. You don't want to wake up one year from a planned retirement date and realize they're too far behind.

From the moment you get married until the day you retire (and beyond), knowing where you stand on your values, goals, and progress is crucial for any healthy partnership.

Home Mortgage vs. Paying Off Student Loans

A couple of years ago, I took a call from a referral through the XY Planning Network — a group of Fee-Only financial planners that cater to Generation X and (Y) Millennials clients. They were a young couple — ages 26-28. I didn't get the specific income figures, but I gathered their household income was around $200,000, which was $150,000 for one person and maybe $50,000 -$70,000 for the partner. They were evaluating whether to take out a substantial loan to use toward buying a house or paying down student debt. There didn't have much regarding investable assets but would consider starting investing. This is a common challenge. They ask, "Well, what do you think we should do? Should we sit down to talk about investments?"

And I responded, "Well, let me give you some things to think about." Remember the assumption: It's not that simple. My friend and mentor, Leanne Kramer, formerly of Ragnar Wealth Management, gave me this advice. Everyone is not your ideal client but always try to leave people in a better position than before they spoke to you, regardless of whether they qualify to be your clients. That stuck with me. **I think the financial services industry misses that sometimes**. That is the definition of reciprocity: No expectation of them becoming a future client but offering a helping hand to people in need, while still respecting the financial planning craft.

The questions I ask always come back to: What do you have, where you want to go, and how you plan to get there?

I also want people to own their decisions based on what they know, how they communicate, and their game plan or process.

With this couple, I started by inquiring about their partnership balance sheet. However, there is an accounting problem related to paying back student loans. Student debt is the liability, but what is the corresponding asset? Intellectual capital doesn't show on the balance sheet. That's a problem. Accountants may respond, "Well, it's not a problem because the asset doesn't exist on the balance sheet, and banks won't loan against it." Well, we're not asking for a loan on our intellectual capital. It's used to gain employment, but there is an undetermined value. I asked, "What's your game plan to address the student loan?" And they responded, "We need to kind of figure it out, and we'd want to reduce it."

I continue, "What's your game plan for the house?"

And then they started telling me about why they like the house and its features. And clearly, there were real estate price appreciation assumptions in there. My response was, "I'm not telling you that you should or shouldn't buy the house. That's not my goal. I think you'll want to get to the central question of *why*." "*Why*" is the whole premise of the home, asset, or hassle process outlined in the "Real Estate" section. These questions are discussion points within your partnership and, most likely, with trusted advisors in mortgages and real estate areas. Several years ago, a real estate agent – Mack McCoy, outlined some questions that couples might face when making real estate and other general financial decisions:

- How do we save up enough for a down payment on a house?
- Should we even save up to put 20% down, or would our cash be better served with a lower down payment and investing the rest?

- How do we buy a house and save for retirement and/or student loans?
- What is the cost to borrow versus the return that we will generate from the house after taxes?

These are additional questions that may factor into your partnership financial decisions.

- What if someone earns a promotion and have to move?
- What if we decide to have kids? That's a whole book in itself.
- What if someone changes careers?
- What if the stock market goes down 25%?
- What if interest rates go up 2% over the next year?
- How is buying or selling personal real estate related to the amount we will need to retire?
- How is the value of real estate related to our overall cash flow and net worth?
- What should we do with our real estate in retirement?
- Should we pay off the mortgage early, and what are the ramifications?
- How do real estate prospects compare to the stock market?
- What should we do if we are getting married and we both own real estate?
- Who pays the mortgage if one of us can't work? Or dies?
- What percentage of our partnership's net worth should we have in our house?
- What are the economic prospects in our local area and our professions?
- How stable are our jobs, and what emergency savings do we or should we have?
- Is there a personal bias towards carrying student debt?
- What is the tax-deductibility of our student loan?

- What is the interest rate on the potential mortgage and the current student loan?
- Is there a forgiveness program offered through our employer or government program?
- Does carrying student debt create negative emotions?
- How long do we plan to live in the house?
- What family dynamics factor into the real estate decision?
- What are the assumptions for furnishing the house?

Ultimately, the discussion should center around:

- Understanding what you have.
- Understanding where you want to go (goals) based on what you have.
- Understanding the strengths and challenges of real estate.
- Consulting a trusted expert if needed.

Mind the Gap

Disclaimer: This section is directed toward audiences outside of engaged and newlywed partnerships at the beginning of their marriage. Other groups include friends, parents, the wedding industry, faith-based organizations, the field of psychology, and the financial services field.

Social Taboo

In recent years, we've broken through a lot of social taboos. When I was growing up, I was taught to avoid discussions regarding sex, race, politics, or religion in social gatherings. Thanks to social media, those walls have been broken through, if not trampled upon entirely. But there remains one conversation that people are very hesitant to talk about: marriage and money.

When I started my Registered Investment Advisory firm in 2015, I tried to identify groups that *really needed my services*, engaged couples consistently fit the bill. If you ask any married couple about their conversations around money, they will tell you it's a top three, if not number one, source of disagreement. If money conversations are such an issue, why don't engaged couples regularly seek third parties to help them through these difficult conversations? Here's why:

- We don't want to find out we are not doing well financially.
- We assume that income equates to financial wellness.
- Some strong cultural norms against money conversations.

- There is a gender bias in the financial services industry that does not cater to women.
- Conversations around money cause anxiety and shame.

If the local economy is doing well, many people tell themselves, "Finances don't matter, everything is going to continue to do well, and we're going to be okay." Partnership income levels that are average and above feel safe and comfortable at their current lifestyle. But is that lifestyle sustainable 30 to 40 years from now? Are we able to keep working at this pace at 60, 70, and 80 years old?

This is why it's important for newlyweds or engaged couples to jumpstart conversations and decisions within their partnership. If we are genuinely interested in preserving relationships and fostering a solid foundation based on communication and trust, then money conversations are essential.

Why are we silent about money? If we (those of us who are married) don't talk about it, then who's going to tell engaged and recently married couples that it takes more than a joint checking account, a funded 401(k), and good FICO scores to have a happy and successful life?

Some programs highlight the challenges of marriage and money. However, I find that they focus on (some might find this paternalistic) regarding budgets, with little connection to the bigger picture. For example, a well-known checklist item is to create a budget. However, with today's couples merging established careers, 401(k)s, real estate, and sometimes business, the budget conversation can be complex. How many distinguish cash flow analysis from a budget and dig deeper into other topics that need more attention to execute a successful plan?

I consulted with a behavioral psychologist regarding why people don't do what they *know* they should do when it comes to money, and she brought up some interesting reasons. She said the power of inertia is nearly unstoppable.

In other words, if the couple hasn't talked about it until now, there isn't a catalyst that will cause them to break this code of communication other than an equal and opposite force, like a major problem. The second reason she suggested is that it usually takes a third party to facilitate these conversations. And third, by nature, we are taught to put out fires, and the only way we deal with these issues is when it causes enough anxiety to force us to act or address something that's gone wrong. However, even when we address these situations, we usually find a short-term solution and get on with our day.

Talking about money is not a life-or-death situation for most people. It's like brushing your teeth after every meal; you know you should do it, most of us don't, and the results don't manifest in the short term. Yet the consequences of not brushing tend to show over the long term.

It's clear there's a knowledge gap when it comes to what we need to address in our total financial picture beyond investments; there are things that we keep hidden not just from the world but from our partners and even ourselves. But there may be a broader, more menacing gap that we should watch out for. On one side of the gap are financially stable partnerships, fully prepared for retirement, and have had all the right money conversations. Couples on the other side of the gap have no idea how to hold money conversations. They have not planned for the future, and they are living day-to-day, paycheck to paycheck, on a short-term or a periodically intermediate-term basis. So how many people occupy each side? My guess is that only a portion of the population has realistic, detailed financial discussions beyond the short term. This guide is designed to help bridge that gap, so all partnerships are on the right side of discussing, planning, and enjoying their entire lives.

The good news is that when talking to Millennials, I hear more proactive conversations about how their financial picture looks together, either before or shortly after marriage.

This book was developed to be a resource for ALL people, regardless of income or net worth. Men, women, domestic partners, business partners, best friends, or siblings, any partnership or relationship can benefit on how to address money conversations.

Parents

For the parents out there, *The Most Valuable Wedding Gift* is about fostering better conversations, better planning, and better decisions. The goal is to be one of the greatest gifts parents can give.

Think back to when you started your partnership. There was probably an uncle, aunt, older brother or sister who sat down with you regarding the first year of marriage. They had some stories to tell! They'd lived it! Think about the first year of your marriage. How was it?

Most smile ruefully, and some share how it's one of the most challenging yet rewarding transitions of their lives. And that journey continues as we incorporate children, career transitions, set up our "Next Chapter," and take care of loved ones (parents) in their final days.

Think about all the concepts you try to pass on to your children. Do they always listen? Can you recall a message delivered more effectively by an outside source despite you saying the exact same thing? Every so often, the value is in the message AND the messenger. Some news is better delivered by someone else.

A lot of your children are successful. They've started a retirement account, they have a brokerage account, some own real estate or businesses, and have benefits. But just as important as all of those "things" is their values system. Here *is a connection between what you value, completing your goals, and how you make your buying, investing, and saving decisions.*

For those who have purchased this book for themselves "to check it out" before gifting, I'll provide support why this could be a valuable wedding gift for your wedding couple.

- Wedding etiquette: Typically, a thank you card is coming your way if you gift this book as a wedding present. This becomes a trigger/reminder that this book is a resource. There's a very high likelihood that the thank you card will include a statement about how they "can't wait to use it."
- When you talk with your newly married child, they'll naturally be reminded of your gift.
- Shocker: in the first year of your child and new in-law's marriage, there will be conflict. There will be things they did not anticipate. They now have a resource ready for them to navigate common marital challenges. This guide was designed to have a long shelf life—we purposefully limited time-sensitive information. We focused on concepts, stories, and analogies to build the foundation and remain relevant. The Most Valuable Wedding Gift can sit on the shelf until needed.

Ideally, it would be great if they both started this course before marriage. Maybe we can soften the message, and it can be incorporated into a pre-marriage counseling and/or faith-based prep session.

This can be your parting gift to them as they transition into their new partnership. Even for those who have left the house years ago, a wedding signifies a departure from the proverbial nest. This gift can be a final helping hand as they transition.

If you're a parent and you have not instilled the concepts that are essential to both creating and maintaining wealth, your children are at risk of falling back. Even those who come from "means" can learn how to discuss finances about and money decisions to maintain their wealth, both in the traditional financial sense and with "off-the-balance sheet" items like values, social capital, and human capital. If I had a dollar for every parent whose child doesn't quite follow the "desired path"—not because of the of their job or career, but because they did not piece it all together— I would own an island or a sports team with an appropriate mascot name. This is an alternative message to children beyond the old mantras of "go to school" and "get a job."

High Shoulder

Of course, the couple has to be ready to receive the message – even as adults, they may give the "high shoulder." Let me explain. The high shoulder is what children will do when they're young, and they want you to show you that they've got it handled. For example, when my children were the ages three and eighteen months of age, we would stop by a store on our way home to pick up a few items. I'd pull the car into the parking lot, turn off the engine, turn off the music, reach back, and say, "Hey, guys. We're about to go in to the store to grab a couple of things, but I need you to do one thing before we get out of the car." And they'd both say, in unison, "Hold my hand." At this point, I think I'm winning because we've talked about this before.

Now the three-year-old is starting to get a little bit more independent, and he says, "Daddy, I don't need to hold your hand. I can walk by myself." Technically, they both could walk. I have to bring my parenting A-game because this is important, right? And even though the 18-month-old isn't talking – he's like S*ri or Al*xa – he's recording everything. And if I don't nail this parenting moment correctly, then two weeks later, I will go through the same thing with Mr. Me Too all over again.

I look back at the three-year-old.

"Look, Mr. Three-feet-high-and-rising, I know you can walk by yourself. In fact, you do a great job of showing your brother how to do it. But in this parking lot, there are cars that *you can't see*, and there are cars that *can't see you*. So, can you help me by holding MY hand so we can both look, and I'll let you hold onto the cart when we get inside?" Whether they're three or thirty-three, when offered help, they may respond, "I got it, I got it."

Except when they don't.

This book is a perfect way to acknowledge that they're successful, that they have great chemistry, and that they're going to have a great partnership. But as a couple, there are some things you may not be able to see lurking around the corner. As a parent, I want to offer this little bit of help, so your children don't have to experience falling down and skinning their knee during those difficult conversations.

To be clear, we're not entirely resolving all their issues, but we can offer a little bit of a helping hand. Exposing your adult child and your new in-laws to components of money conversations early in their partnership can address the "I got it, I got it" that turns into "I need help!"

Seasoned Partners

A question I often receive is: Would this program help couples who are already married? The answer is yes, but I would be remiss if I did not state that these concepts are best exposed, learned, and incorporated earlier in the relationship rather than later. If not, it's like trying to pick up a foreign language later in life.

For example:

A couple of years ago, I was sitting at a local St∗rb∗cks enjoying a purchased coffee with the strong accompanying WiFi. Using the table as an office, I was reviewing a video of myself talking about Marriage & Money for post-video production purposes. A woman approached me from behind and asked if I was watching a video of myself. I'll admit, I was a little caught off guard because that was *exactly* what I was doing. I felt guilty and a little bit narcissistic, but when I told her about the topic of money conversations, her curiosity turned to excitement as I outlined the purpose of the program.

I highlighted that *The Most Valuable Wedding Gift* was about both the *how* and the *what* regarding money conversations, and ultimately about how we can make decisions in a partnership. She completely confirmed my assumptions and was raving about how much we needed this. After several minutes of talking, we both had to go; I told her that I'm still fine-tuning the behavior content. I offered to send her a copy of the video for her partnership (together for eight years) in exchange for their feedback.

And the look on her face went from delightfully curious to mortified in the space of three seconds.

Her eyes dropped, and she murmured:

"I don't think so........my partner and I can't even have this conversation."

That hit me like a punch to my stomach. She'd been with her partner for over eight years, but this would be a complete nonstarter for them. As I started telling other people about this project, I received more and more people—even in their partners' presence—telling me that they LOVED the idea. Still, money conversations were so difficult that they regularly avoided the topic. For those who have been in a partnership for five, ten, even twenty years, what would the value be of laying the foundation for money conversations at the beginning? What time, energy, emotions, sleep, and opportunities are sacrificed due to less than ideal money conversations within a partnership?

Honestly, this has driven me to produce this book, so I can make an impact with my family, friends, community, and people I will never meet. If I do this right, helping shape money conversations may be my legacy.

The Wedding Industry

Why am I attempting to partner with the wedding industry? Well, your former clients are my prospective students. After the vows and the dancing and the sparklers, they start the clock on their "forever after" journey together. Just as your marketing goal shifts from offering client services to remain at the top of your former clients' minds, *The Most Valuable Wedding Gift* offers the perfect resource along with other "nice to have" resources that may arise during your relationship.

Money conversations aren't a manufactured challenge. What couple *doesn't* struggle with financial conversations early in their partnership? It's tough to talk about money and make financial decisions as a couple. The simple truth is, couples need help.

Some people in the wedding industry view this as something that has no place in the wedding process. My goal is not to tell people how much to spend on the wedding, which is not my job, responsibility, or intention. But do partnership communication, understanding value systems, social capital related to goals, and human behavior with financial resources relate to the wedding?

Some in the wedding industry see the value, and we truly appreciate the honesty. What is the true value of *The Most Valuable Wedding Gift* to the partnership - if received early and correctly? What is the cost of this book? The difference between the two *is* the gift.

We have all heard, "Here's my cell number; give me a call if you need anything." If you've said this and meant it, then you are precisely the professional who will appreciate this program because your clients are more than just a number to you.

Additional Concepts of Value That Align with Money Conversations

If a couple has a hard time listening to one another during the wedding planning stage, it may be an indicator they will have trouble listening when it comes time to discuss money, values, and planning after they make it down the aisle.

You already recommend great wedding venues/caterers/photographers to your clients (to build your value and gain their trust). *Marriage & Money* is an enduring service that will outlast all the day-of referral vendors.

Having a financial discussion/plan early on may give the couple a chance to find alternate ways to pay for their wedding.

They may have another wedding to plan/pay for in the future: their child's.

Part of your services could/should focus on "what's next?" or "post-wedding" planning.

You can cultivate a new value-add as to why they should select you as their vendor: you even provide them with resources for after the "big day."

· You can offer this "gift of knowledge" to any couple, regardless of their faith or background.

Faith-Based Groups

Other groups that I hope acknowledges the value of money conversations are faith-based groups. Faith-based groups and churches offer complete life advice. They are beacons for their membership in all aspects of life. Shouldn't that journey include personal finance values, goals, and how to get there? These organizations are in the perfect position to offer resources to the engaged and newly married couples in the congregation.

Devout faith-based members often complete premarital counseling at their place of worship or with their faith-based leaders. This counseling typically involves all aspects of marriage (the good and the bad). Couples get an idea of what to expect and how to handle things from sex, religious practice, children, education, fidelity, family, friends, and even diet. While these are authentic challenges that new couples face, issues with money conversations also rank just as high, if not higher, as marital challenges. Faith-based counselors can genuinely help couples not only succeed in their marriage but to be happy.

If the topic of money comes up in a premarital counseling session, are couples given comprehensive financial roadmap that they can carry with them for the rest of their lives? There are so many aspects of money conversations (life goals, values, retirement plans, and how to address it all as a partnership), it would be impossible to cover them all in counseling. These are conversations that many of us wish we had in our early years of marriage. If there is anybody we would listen to about these topics, it would be our faith-based leaders. Seasoned couples clearly can also benefit as organizations ask for tithes and donations from their congregation.

Marital Therapists and Counseling Community

Similar to faith-based organizations, therapists, and counselors helping people navigate multiple aspects of their lives. More specifically, areas that present challenges within relationships. We understand that the topic of money conversations is tough to tackle for everyone. For some of us, money conversations sit right between finance and psychology, but due to the wall of silence, we may fail to bridge the gap to connect these aspects of our lives. But if there's a group who can help couples out by addressing marital troubles, it's psychology. Not only are you equipped to give life advice, but clients are likely to *follow* that advice. It could be helpful for both therapists and clients to have a program like this as a resource.

I am not offering personalized advice – counseling, therapy, or financial—the goal of this book is to expose and raise awareness regarding common elements that impact our partnership money conversations. Like 99% of financial professionals, my goal is not to attempt to solve people's marital problems. And that's where our roles are different. It's a small but an important distinction. *The Most Valuable Wedding Gift* is designed to address -what I believe - is a primary determinant in making better personal and partnership decisions.

The Financial Services Community

I consider my professional family those who offer personalized financial services to individuals – including partnerships. This includes financial advisors, planners, insurance agents, CPAs, enrolled agents, bankers, real estate agents, and estate planners. My goal with this guide is to give you a helping hand. As someone who's worked closely with professionals in the areas mentioned above, I know how difficult your job is. You are asked to perform at a high level – sometimes without the benefit of solid communication, SMART goals, and articulated value systems, and with the negative impact of some human behaviors.

If you could address these issues in one place for newlyweds, would you?

While the wedding doesn't seem like a natural place for your services, I propose this. If you gift this to your clients who have children that are getting married soon – what is the upside? They are prepared with the hard part of gathering the appropriate information. How would a parent feel if you exposed them to something they wish they had received?

The Elephant and the Giraffe

As professionals, we can all do a better job for our couples around preparing them for money conversations. It's like elephants and giraffes in the safari. We all go to the same watering hole. Maybe we eat some of the same plants, but we don't interact despite threats from the outside. It's not as if we are feuding like the Hatfield's and McCoy's or Kayne West and Taylor Swift. Instead of just coexisting, we could collaborate for the sake of the couples we all serve.

•

Partnership Wedding Planner

WP: Wedding Planner (age 30-40), Confident and established

P1: Engaged partner (early 30s)

P2: Engaged partner (early 30s)

The scene at Coffee Shop or Living Room

The wedding planner is checking off items on her To-Do-List.

WP: Let's review our wedding to-do-list, shall we? Flowers for the wedding party? Check. Cake colors? Check. Valet parking? Check.

P1 & P2 nod, and WP reads off of a sheet.

WP: (Putting the list down) Now, remember how I promised our wedding planning service really is one-of-a-kind? While other wedding planners are done at the end of your reception....we go the extra step. Here's our special Checklist for the days AFTER your special day.

WP hands them an envelope.

P2: That's cool.

P1: (reading the sheet) Thank you cards (nods in approval), adding names to car insurance, updating benefits through work (nods). The Most Valuable wedding gift? (Looking up from sheet to Wedding Planner, perplexed.)

P1: What?

P2: Huh?

WP: Look, I've been doing this for a while…..money is the #1 cause of stress in a relationship for couples, but it doesn't have to be……the gift is a guide for money conversations. So everyone can be on the same page.

P1: (Nervous laugh) But we don't have money problems. We both have good jobs; we even have our own 401(k)'s.

WP: Which is exactly why you need to address all of the "stuff" you don't have, which is your joint cash flow, blended balance sheet, identified values, life insurance, tax planning, and our human behaviors that can create a challenge regarding money and other "stuff." These days, working professionals have more complexities than 30-40 years ago.

P2: Sounds important.

P1: Sound complicated; I mean…..we don't even know where to start….

WP: Well, it can start with both of you creating this roadmap regarding money conversations that affect your everyday lives, a roadmap to money conversations regarding stuff your parents never tell you before marriage but critical to…."

P2: (Cuts her off) I think I heard about this. It's this financial guy who talks about money with other relationship stuff. He goes over the numbers AND communication. He just lays it out there without the investment/insurance sale pitch.

P1: Just a roadmap?

WP: Just a roadmap.

P2: A checklist for "forever after." You really **do** go above and beyond...."

Social Values

People often ask about the backstory of the *Marriage & Money* program. To be honest, there isn't one single story that lead me to put this book together. Rather, it was a LONG journey of realizations about the relationship between money, communication, and behavior when addressing partnerships versus individuals.

One of the first defining moments during my time building my financial planning practice was identifying my niche. The people who chose to work with me were what I call "baby baby boomers": people in their mid-50s or early 60s, born anywhere between 1962 and 1968. They asked me to help build a plan for them as they approached their Do-What-You-Want period over the upcoming three to seven years.

As I spoke to them and evaluated their situation, many of them understandably, had other concerns. One of their concerns was around their adult children. The adult kids were out of the house with solid careers and were starting to get married. Yet the parents were concerned that the kids really didn't have a solid grip on their overall finances. They asked me if I could give their kids a head start as they entered their new partnership. At the time, I searched for any guides or roadmaps that could offer them a helping hand. As it turns out, I didn't see too many comprehensive resources for the 30-something year-olds getting married to help them with "stuff" like careers, retirement plans, properties, established money values, or even businesses/side-hustles. A lot of these articles—let's say 4 out of 5—are about getting out of debt and joint versus separate bank accounts. And, of course, I think that's important. Yet there's a large swath of people who don't need a lot of emphasis on debt management or credit-card use, but they still need financial help!

There's a gap!

Those on one side of the gap are spending a lot less than they earn, and when they get to the Do-What-You-Want period, they're likely going to be fine. Then you have those on the other side who are living at the margins, or caught up in consumption, who are going to need a lot of help when it comes to financial management. Then, there's a group in between, sort of like the ignored middle child, or middle America, that, at times, may feel neglected between the coasts. It can be a challenge to find them, to identify their needs, and to present resources that are helpful beyond putting money in a jar.

That's why I launched this program. People, specifically young couples, can benefit from information that they know they don't know AND what they don't know they don't know - especially early on. There's tons of information shared about different aspects of finances, but few are talking about the bigger picture. We want to set young couples up with the knowledge they need to be financially comfortable in spending, saving, and communicating. This can help reduce many concerns they may have later as they approach their later years and the Do-What-You-Want period.

This book is not about finding financial planning clients for me. In fact, I purposely wrote this book using my +20 years of experience but hopefully giving you more than the typical half answers. It's about giving those couples the know-how and confidence to make money decisions down the road. The success of *The Most*

Valuable Wedding Gift would mean I've reached people in different parts of the country who may not have need or desire for full financial planning services but needed help to fill in the gaps. Or maybe they even work with an advisor currently but now expect a higher level of service.

When we're at that age at which we're transitioning to being on our own, we are generally not prepared for the complexities of partnership finances. We're taught to believe that as long as we go to college and stay out of credit card debt, we'll be able to fund the rest of our lives: marriage, a house, a car, kids, the whole nine. While we all know that this isn't necessarily the reality, are we as a society doing anything to change that mindset? We need to teach young couples and young adults that a college education alone may not be enough to set your partnership up for the perfect future.

We have a generation of people who lack general financial acumen and confidence to properly manage their entire lives. With the current pandemic, we can start to recognize what happens to a generation when the economy goes south. The expectation is that things should be fine and they aren't. A segment of people will play the blame game regarding who's responsible. There will be a lot of finger-pointing at various groups of people, but little responsibility regarding their own planning and preparedness. We've seen this before and it's not good.

I'm concerned about what might happen in the near future when people are angry about their current financial situation and are assessing blame.

However, if we can just deliver the right information to the people who need it the most, when the economy takes a hit, we'll be in better shape. Again, let's focus on what we can control.

Married Life: A Partnership

Marriage & Money addresses the behavioral aspect of finances, instead of just various investment products, and specifically evaluates the decision- making process and what can help them to identify challenges in their journey together.

Generally speaking, when people get married, they will make some changes. We've all heard stories of people who've lived together for a long time before deciding to get married because they had already settled into a pattern of managing the household. Well, things continue to change throughout our lives, whether we like it or not. Couples could live together, and make all these decisions together, for years. But once they are married, for the majority of people, things will be different.

But what if we could catch people at that point of crossing over into married life, into a new partnership? I think there's a huge advantage to that. Generally speaking, the longer people are married, the more they are set in their ways. Trying to change the financial habits of an established married couple is like trying to teach my grandmother about Facebook. It might be interesting, but is she really going to embrace change?

Therefore, I tried to find a strategic entry point - where people are receptive to these changes and can carry them out and benefit from them over the long haul.

Social Change

Another challenge I want to address on a bigger scale is creating social change. I believe there is significant social value to teaching financial literacy. It's something that's a sensitive topic, but the reality is that much of this information on handling money is not widely available or not presented in a way that is helpful or digestible.

What often happens is that one person in a partnership has some of this information. The other partner is like, "Okay, well, they seem to know what to do here, so I'll just ride along." Ride or decide. And yet there's this disconnect, because while one person is in charge of the finances (like paying household bills), a lot of other decisions (such as individual spending) are made by the other party. Neither sees the big picture of partnership finances that's being painted as two people are making decisions on a day-to-day basis.

I think there's a whole swath of our society that still haven't been in the right place to get this trickle-down information, whether it's because of their gender or ethnicity or because they simply do not have the investable assets for higher-level planning.

There is one thing I don't want to understate, but I also want to say it very, very carefully. The goal of *Marriage and Money* is to expose and deliver financial concepts to everyone across all partnerships. I do not want to come across as patronizing and condescending to women and minorities. I simply want to address the disconnect between all groups that need to move forward financially.

Do we need to see better financial management in the partnership structure? The answer is "yes." But it's not an easy issue to address.

In a study for Merrill Lynch, Wave Age found that 61% of women would rather talk about their eventual death than money. [Wave Age. 2018] That's not good. To be clear, there are women doing great work specifically *for* women. Also, there's an active effort in the financial planning industry to attract more female financial planners. But my approach, this program, isn't just about females, or males for that matter. It's about the PARTNERSHIP, which includes a demographic that's currently underserved. This isn't a continuation of how things have always been done. We're swimming in a different direction with a different approach that, hopefully, will yield different results.

When we talk about some of the challenges, some of the barriers that exist, I hope people realize that I KNOW those barriers exist for women and communities of color. I also know that the barriers may not be the same for everyone. I just want ALL people to have access to this information. They can decide what they want to do with it, but if they don't have the information, we've limited their choices. Bottom line: our goal is to level the playing field.

To be clear, I'm not completely blaming any establishment for this uneven distribution of knowledge. **Regardless of how people identify themselves, we, including myself, are all responsible for our decisions.** The outcome may include factors outside of our control but the decisions are ours. This applies to all couples— whether traditional or same-sex. It's about making decisions for the greater good of the partnership while maintaining the individual components.

This is so important for young, newly married people—just as they begin their partnership. We as friends and family hope we can connect with them early because we all know that once life begins to take over, we are focusing on the now versus the intermediate and long-term. For most, the importance of getting serious about money conversations, planning, and behavior is undeniable. But then we insert our "we'll do it when we aren't as busy," or "when we buy our first house," or "when we run into trouble," "when we feel like we are ready" and guess what? You'll look up 10 to15 years later – and realize that you need to make major changes. Only now it's much more difficult. Like going back to school after spending time in the workforce: it's difficult.

Lee Eisenberg's book *The Number: What Do You Need for the Rest of Your Life, and What will Cost You"* calls it *the lost years*. This is where we are just living our life and making the most of our decisions in the short term with a few decisions that are intermediate-term. The results are not much progress regarding reaching our financial goals. I wouldn't say those years are lost but I would describe them as the "spinning" years. It's like treading water. We're aware of where we are and we are doing a lot but it's like we are in the middle of a spinning class; we're doing all this pedaling but aren't really going anywhere. Little progress is made towards long-term goals. That is why *now* is important. The sooner we can learn about the things that will affect us later, the more prepared we will be to handle them when the time comes. This is why I decided to focus on the timeframe of the wedding or shortly after.

Even though money conversations absolutely impact decisions couples make, including the wedding, we don't specifically address the budget of the big day. We're not saying, "Hey, you're spending too much money on the wedding." That would be imposing my values on couples' decisions. Instead, we ask "Do you want to have better money conversations, less stress, and make better choices going forward, forever after?" We use the tagline *Planning For Forever After* because your partnership could/should last a VERY long time. Still, some focus so much time and energy on planning the actual wedding: many for more than a year! And of course, there's a lot of money involved in that. But when you say, "Hey, let's allocate TEAM resources toward the actual marriage starting on day one" people freeze up, because there's a disconnect.

That's why this book is also designed for parents or other family or friends to give as a gift. As someone who cares about the couple's happiness, the approach is to give our couple this gift. It may not be glamorous, tangible, or even sentimental, but it's something they're going to need. A lot of times, it's just not urgent to the couple getting married and challenges arise shortly after. That's a problem.

Building a Knowledge Base

We want people to be more knowledgeable, so that when we work with them, or other advisors work with them, they come in with a better knowledge base. And then we can be more effective in our practice.

If you have ever talked to a wedding planner, they're at their best when everybody's on board, and there's a clear line of communication, and every knows their role. That works better than having to reestablish roles, troubleshoot communication, and revisit the entire wedding planning process.

We want people to raise the bar for themselves, so they come in prepared, and so we (financial advisors/planners) can deal with these complex issues a lot more effectively. Can we set a higher level of expectation within the financial advice field? We'll see.

There's another aspect worth mentioning as I look out into the future. And it's really played out over the last several years. See, we have a group of people—and it's not just in one part of the country—who are approaching the middle of their career and their retirement. And they have an expectation of what retirement will look like and who will provide for it. And sometimes those expectations aren't met. So my other reason for doing this is to really try to move the needle and help people take responsibility for their financial future. There may be some outside financial help out there, like Social Security, but ultimately, it's on ourselves.

That responsibility takes planning. My fear is that if the next generation isn't ready, and their expectations aren't met, people will point fingers. We've seen this plenty of times, in a variety of forms. And we know how it plays out. So I want to do my part to help that pointing finger do a 180 degree turn, to transition people to saying, "Okay, now I'm responsible and here is what can I do about it." I want people to have the dialogue, to create the roadmap. To help them lay the foundation for success, to be prepared, to find the right financial advisor, to make better decisions, and not be so angry. When people get angry, they have a tendency to point fingers, right?

If I could help those groups, even people who really don't agree with everything I say or identify with me personally, then I've done everything I can do.

If I'm completely honest, I'm really concerned about a large group of people moving toward a phase of life they're not ready for. They're not ready for retirement. They're not ready for a career change. They're not ready for the family component. And my concern is that fingers will point and blame assigned, and again, we've seen how that works out. I don't want that. I'm sure that politicians do what they can. And I'm doing my part by saying, "Look, just let me try to make a difference through my profession and this program." Because there are benefits to financial literacy that go far beyond just making more money.

How Marriage & Money is different

People ask us how Marriage & Money is different than other programs. Originally, I would make comments about specific noted personal finance experts. Generally, my comments were positive as we're better off by having these resources. But the *Marriage & Money* program along with the this book *The Most Valuable Wedding Gift* is different in several important ways.

First, most other money-and-marriage programs—focuses almost exclusively on budgeting and debt management. So much so that you would think money conversations are all about budgeting, credit scores, and debt management. That's actually less than 25% of of our focus. Which leads us to who benefits from *The Most Valuable Wedding Gift*.

Second, we have a younger and different financial demographic. Some have stock options, business interests, real estate, and family dynamics … thus there's added complexity. Our couples do have budget conversations, but they do not carry overwhelming debt, so we look at other things. Because money conversations are so much more than budgets.

Third, every expert has their own experience – but the Marriage & Money program includes content from licensed and certified professionals from the field of finance and psychology. Instead of solving for one goal, in real life we address multiple goals like retirement, running a business, and adult continuing education at the same time. You want someone familiar with the tax system and qualified plan structures to provide a sound, well rounded perspective. And calling people stupid and an idiot may be entertaining to some but simply **not** professional.

Finally, I've noticed almost all the other programs impose their value system. Statements telling the reader what they **must or need to do**. We want to recognize money values but not dictate them to partnerships. Our job is to provide perspective supported by statistics and highlight multiple scenarios so couples can discuss, evaluate, and make decisions that are appropriate for them.

Financial Plan –Input

Some people assume financial planning only has to do with the numbers. At the end of the day, the algorithms financial professionals produce are only as good as the information they receive. If you're sitting down with a financial advisor in their office, the exchange of information could go beyond bank statements and tax returns. Beyond the financials, let me share with you the information I gather when I meet with partnerships for the first time.

Interest

First, I start with this question: "What do you like to do for fun?" And I let people talk. Almost every partnership I sit down with gives me "the look" that says that's not a financial question, so why are you asking? After a couple of moments, one person starts to smile and lays out what they enjoy. It's interesting to see how the two interact when describing the activities, they enjoy and how often they do or would like to do them. One aspect that can be challenging, not only for myself but also for many people in financial services, is listening and letting them talk. Because we are trained to give information and not so much to listen.

Additionally, I can't tell you how many times a partnership sits down for a financial planning session, and one person does all the talking. And the other person sits back and listens and chimes in once or not at all. We're not always looking for an equal contribution, but I think it's crucial for both people to feel like it's their plan. It's a partnership plan and not one for just one person dictating all of the inputs.

Goals

Then I move away from interests and ask them to provide their goals. Again, I let people talk. In this book, we describe S.M.A.R.T. goals, but my in-person meetings are not a goal-making class. I just let them go. Sometimes I have to remind them that they aren't restricted to financial goals. Goals could be anything, like learning to garden or playing the guitar or even tutoring local school kids. It's their goals. In my experience, most partnerships do not schedule a time for conversations of this type. It's eye-opening for couples who've been together for +20 years to recognize that this exercise is new and valuable to their partnership.

I clarify that there are short-term, long-term, and intermediate-term goals. If the goals seem involved, then I may ask if they have an accountability partner.

Values

Then we get to "the big one": What are their values? Sitting down and talking about it with someone is entirely different than filling in an online form about values. Maybe it's a generational thing, but I would imagine that most people feel that this is where human interaction comes in.

Trusted Advisors

The next thing I ask: who are the other people that are important to them. Who are their trusted advisors? Maybe it's someone who's a business partner or anybody else of significance that they want to incorporate into their plan. Most people assume I'm just dealing with investments, stocks, bonds, insurance, and mutual funds. But the reality is that there are typically other advisors in someone's life, people like CPAs, estate planners, attorneys, insurance people, lending people, real estate people, or a family member who influences other aspects of their financial lives and how they make decisions.

Process

Then we talk about their process. How do they make decisions? Frequently, this is an eye-opening inquiry because they realize they don't have a process, or if they do, it's loose and informal. Some people make a decision by talking with a trusted friend. Some people need to feel comfortable with the downside or worst-case scenario before they can take any action. Others need to explore every angle and feel like they've dissected every alternative. Still others use third-party verification through professional sources or research. It fascinates me that, in general, people don't do more work on their decision-making process. I think it makes for better decisions and for understand mistakes and corrective measures.

Joint Cash Flow and Blended Balance Sheet

Finally, I usually end with a discussion about assets, liabilities, and cash flow. Some people come prepared with their numbers, and some people don't. It's the financial planner/advisor's responsibility to give both of you (both of you!) a level of comfort with your current numbers, the projections, and account for potential variability in income because many partnerships will have varying cash flow. When you start to dive into this, you find there are a lot of feelings and emotions involved.

The Financial Roadmap

A realistic and effective financial plan has several key components. As you put your plan together, you'll decide that some components don't concern you right now. But it's still good idea to address them in the beginning because they may factor into your overall financial picture in the future. Too many times, I see the simplified version without an actual "real plan" behind it. Having notes on an index card is convenient, but many partnerships deal with decisions that may require more than a 3x5 card.

First, just from an operational standpoint, I think it makes sense to create a **table of contents** or **executive summary**, which outlines where the rest of these pieces can be found. The financial plan isn't something people view every day, so it helps to have a way of finding data quickly.

You also want to have the **statement of cash flow** and the **statement of financial position** for your partnership. In other words, your joint income statement; and then your partnership net worth statement or blended balance sheet. Those are the two pillars of your financial plan. Without them, it's like building a house without the blueprints.

Next, it's important to outline **assumptions**, such as **inflation, growth rates** and **interest rates**. Mortgage rates are relatively static, but other interest rates change over time, both pre-retirement and post-retirement.

And **goals:** We talk about the relationship between values, goals, and products. Then the action will be a decision or behavior. We also want to address adult educational goals specifically or any type of funds to help achieve it. It doesn't necessarily have to equate to money. It could be time and energy to acquire the skills or knowledge you want to obtain going forward.

Then you have your **emergency fund**: funds coming from savings versus investing and various percentages.

Many times, **risk** is addressed through insurance. But actually, for anything you have or plan to have, Review the "risk-return" section on choices related to risk.

Also aligned with risk is **consumer debt management**. If you have student loans or credit card debt, all that should be outlined because they're related to your actions and your blended balance sheet.

Your portfolio would include **investments**. This could include stocks, bonds, mutual funds, or retirement account or other marketable securities. It's not just what you have, but also where the investments are going known through a target allocation, and any characteristics in evaluating those investments and retirement goals realistically.

Any goal of **home purchase** would be in there as well. Also, any **estate planning** needs such as having - a will, a financial power of attorney and a P.O.A. for health care, and any health care directives.

If you're starting a **business** or you already have a significant business ownership component, you want to address that in your financial plan, too.

Finally, think about any **family dynamics** that could positively or negatively affect your financial plan. It may sound "extra" or feel uncomfortable, but it can make your plan more realistic.

If you're putting a financial plan together yourself, I think it's always helpful to cover all of these areas. If you're working with a third party, there are five additional aspects you may want to request.

#1: Disclaimer. Be sure you understand the area they are speaking about and any assumptions made as outlined in the beginning. Understand the context and the situation in which the information is provided because it could make a world of difference.

#2: Letter of engagement. We're not dealing with a transactional type of relationship. It's very important to understand the services your professional is providing and what you're paying for those services. It's important to understand what those services are and how you actually receive them.

#3: Explanation of the financial planning process. Identifying what you have, where you want to go, and how you're going to get there.

#4: Recommendations. You don't have to take them all, but it makes sense to have those outlined very clearly after going through all this. What are the recommended next steps?

#5: Conflicts of interest. Is there any third-party compensation to the person providing you with the advice?

These are the components of a complete financial plan. Your financial situation is unique and complex. One-off discussions about your retirement plan are nice, but they may not be enough to take you where you want to be financially within your partnership. Sit down together, discuss and map out your plan.

Joint bank account vs Separate bank accounts

"Should we blend our bank accounts or keep them separate?"

This is a primary question associated with the topic of marriage & money. It seems like a simple question that leads to a simple solution, but I'm going to put this in the category of: it depends.

The Flow of Money:

Flow of Money for Partnership

	Partner A	Joint Partnership	Partner B
Source of Income			
Employer			
Business			
Rent			
Checking Account			
Outflow			
Spending			
Saving			
Investing			

Money or income from an outside source (Employer, business income or rents) to partnership checking account(s).

Money from checking account(s) flows out to current expenses, savings, and investments. We'll assume:

- Any charitable donations are investments into social capital.
- We are not receiving passive income from investments.
- Selling investments is generally not considered a repeatable source of income.
- Any money left in the account at the end of the period is considered savings.

Reminder: this is a partnership.

Option #1: Traditional model. One source of income, one joint checking account, covers all expenses, savings, and investments for the partnership.

Option #1: Traditional Model

	Partner A	Joint Partnership	Partner B
Source of Income			
Employer	☐		
Business			
Rent			
Checking Account		☐	
Outflow			
Spending			
Saving			
Investing			

Pros: Simplicity

Cons: Potentially, the partner who earns the income feels entitled to decisions regarding how money is spent, saved, and invested. What is a *potential* problem?   In the decision section, we highlighted that some decisions could benefit one partner and not the other.

Example: clothing purchases.

Is the partnership agreeable to how decisions are made related to savings and investing, forgoing current consumption for future consumption?

Option #2: Keep everything separate. This applies when both parties have a source of income.

Option #2: Keep Everything Separate

	Partner A	Joint Partnership	Partner B
Source of Income			
Employer	☐		☐
Business			
Rents			
Checking Account	☐		☐
Outflow			
Spending	☐	???	☐
Saving		???	
Investing		???	

Pro: Simple if both parties earn similar incomes and cover needs/want in the short, intermediate, and long term.

Arguments for this model: "I don't want the other partner – or anyone for that matter – telling me how to spend, save, or invest **my money.**" Or I earn it, I burn it.

Con: This model does not explicitly account for decisions (spending, savings, and investing) that benefit both parties. Are retirement funds for one party or two? Should the savings amount cover the future unexpected expense of one partner or two? Some expenses are ambiguous as to who is the primary consumer.

Example: who uses Netflix the most (unless the partnership is in *Netflix and chill* mode). Who pays for dinner when dining out. Clearly, gender, age, and cultural roles factor in how this is set up. Again, if partners are treated equally, and both incomes are similar, it's typically not a problem. The problems may arise when values systems conflict.

Also, planning for the D.W.Y.W. (Do-What-You-Want) period. Earlier in the titling section, we referenced that financial institutions have guidelines regarding how they treat partnerships. For example, the ability to use an IRA. is dependent on partnership income, not individual income, despite the fact that IRA's, by definition, are individual vehicles, not partnership vehicles. Joint IRA's do not exist. − *Maybe they should.

Generally speaking, financial professionals like financial advisors and accountants rely on coordinating within the partnership. Proactive planning is very difficult when operating separately.

Option #3: Hybrid. Earnings from all outside sources flow into individual separate checking accounts, and each person contributes an amount that goes into a joint partnership checking account to pay for joint expenses. Or all earnings flow through a joint checking account, and a system is established on how funds are allocated from joint to separate checking accounts for individual spending, savings, and investment.

Option #3: Hybrid

	Partner A	Joint Partnership	Partner B
Source of Income			
Employer	[　　　]		[　　　]
Business			
Rents			
Checking Account	[　　　]		[　　　]
Outflow			
Spending	[　　　]	%	[　　　]
Saving	[　　　]	%	[　　　]
Investing	[　　　]	%	[　　　]

Question: Does it make it easy for operation and decision-making? If we assume basic needs are covered, what is the point of contention? What if someone wants to spend $100 on an item that isn't valued by the other partner? In option #1, there should be clear communication regarding what items requires approval/conversation **and** at what dollar amount: The elephant in the room. Some (maybe many) people marrying later (after mid-twenties) in life feel a certain expectation of "my" money. There's a sense of freedom with making independent financial choices, even inside a partnership. People telling other people how to spend their money doesn't always go over well.

However, some people – again, coming from an independent background – feel they independently brought the money in, so independently, they should be able to take (spend) the money out. The key is to have a conversation/discussion to come to a mutual understanding of how decisions fit financially AND decisions make each of the partners feel. Belief systems matter. History with money matters. Emotions matter.

Let's assume the partnership household income is $12,000/month or roughly $150,000/year when factoring in bonuses. One $250 unexpected purchase is a small dent when it comes to the overall financial journey. However, an *aggregation* of small purchases of $50, $70, $150, $350, or $1,000 will derail even modest plans to achieve intermediate and long-term goals.

When things are not communicated clearly upfront and expectations aren't met, there is a potential for animosity to build regarding the allocation percentage of individual money from individual income to pay for joint spending, saving, and investing. For example, two people who have similar incomes, but only one person pays the mortgage despite both names being on the title and the mortgage. Or the partnership has a short term rental, and one partner is responsible for all the bookings, cleaning, and customer service questions. How is that accounted for regarding time, energy, and ability?

In addition, when circumstances change, and there isn't an adjustment, it can create additional challenges. For example, let's say someone receives a raise or stops working for a company to start their own business or go back to school. Or let's just say, in general, someone disagrees with the proportion of expenses based on income. What if one source of income is uneven like people who work in sales? How does the adjustment work? These questions should be addressed at the beginning of the relationship when things are not contentious.

Some might think this isn't a big deal in the first year, that they will "figure it out." But let's observe the potential impact. On one hand, someone feels that they are paying a larger percentage of their income for joint living expenses. Is that fair? Someone else might feel that living expenses are shared regardless, so why not agree on what expenses should be shared?

What about savings and investments or otherwise known as future expenses? Who is responsible?

What if one partner works and the other is in school or at home with children?

How should expenses, especially wants, discretionary, non-essential decisions, be made within the partnership?

These are challenging but meaningful conversations and decisions that can benefit the partnership going forward.

Advanced: Loose Language

This is an advanced topic but helpful when applied to partnership conversations and decisions.

Active listening, active **reading**, confirming what was said, and incorporating emotions all matter. In this section, we will explore how the words we use can materially impact both our conversation and decisions. I call this "loose language." This can mean a variety of things from:

- omitting components of a statement critical to a conversation and making a decision
- substituting words that sound similar
- changing the meaning or the same word can have different meanings for different people.

I didn't take this section from any standardized test, but maybe I should have paid more attention in English class.

For example, most people understand the difference between the words "possibility" and "probability." "Possibility" describes the scenario – what could happen.

"Probability" gives a level of confidence or likelihood something will happen. Probability can be expressed in a percentage or words expressing percentage. Technically, the chance is greater than zero. For example:

- Likely ~ 50% or greater
- Unlikely ~less than 50%

- Reasonable ~ above a low percentage (low is subjective and can range from 10% to 30%, depending on the circumstance)
- Probably ~ above 60%
- Confident ~ above 70%

Let's apply this to everyday situations.

A common phrase is: "I don't want to take any risk."

Well, it's tough to live in a world where you don't accept any risk. If you leave the house, you will accept some type of risk. Actually, staying in bed incurs risk. There are very, very few guarantees in life.

Or you might hear, "I don't want to do X, because Y might happen."

I don't want to invest in the stock market because I might lose money.

I don't want to go to that neighborhood because I might become a victim of crime.

These statements clearly outline that scenario Y *could* happen, but what is said about Y's probability? Likely? Reasonable? Probable? Confident?

The probability component is undefined - without implying beyond what was said.

Possibility and probability are different. Going back to risk assessment, we often have to make tough choices about accepting risk, reducing risk, transferring risk, or completely avoiding or eliminating risk. If Y scenario has a downside risk level of less than 1% or .01% or even once in known history- should you avoid it? Should you bypass the opportunity?

This is a very important concept when having tough conversations and making difficult decisions.

When approaching certain groups about addressing money conversations early in a partnership - a common mindset is: Don't bring up the subject of money conversations before marriage. If they read it, they may not go through with the wedding.

Most people will acknowledge there is a possibility for a partnership that reading a book on money conversations can delay or even cause the wedding to be called off. That is a possibility.   What is the probability? I'll simply ask: Have you ever personally known or heard **first-hand** of money discussions ruining a wedding?

I'll wait.

Reference point, there were over 2 million marriages in the U.S. in 2019. And if a money conversation delay or cancel a wedding – what was the underlying cause? The book about money conversations OR other underlying factors, such as their different value systems, emotional impact, lack of communication? All of these are covered earlier in this book.

"What *could happen"* describes the scenario. *Would* imply a *more than likely outcome*.

In an emotional conversation, what happens when "could" is replaced with "would" or even "should"? One letter can change the whole meaning of a word, sentence, and conversation. What if communication is through email or text? Autocorrect is famous for occasionally auto-mistaking.

Moving on to the same word, different definitions. As a finance person, I'm aware of basic words and their meanings, but I've uncovered that I've created my own definition for basic words.

For example, until five years ago, the meaning of the word "amazing" to me: something in the top 5% or higher. My value scale for these words are:

Good   80% - 90%
Great   90% - 100%
Amazing 95% -100%

Therefore, if I was told something was amazing, I was expecting something in the top percentile. When I looked up the definition of amazing, the definition referred to *surprise, astonishment, or wonder*.   Applying that definition to a service or product, "amazing" refers to *surpassing expectations*.

Therefore, by definition, a stock return could be amazing because it surpassed expectations but fell in the 80% range regarding value – less than "my" definition of amazing.   To further complicate communication, what if someone sets my expectation at "amazing"? Now my expectation is set higher, and thus it is harder for it to be amazing due to my elevated standard.

Some of you are thinking, "Roderick, you are two test questions away from being E.S.L." Others will recognize that words matter. Emotions aside, two people using the same word with different definitions can lead to a disconnect in conversations regarding money conversations and decisions.

Advanced: Fallacies

Fallacies are holes in our logic. These examples are not designed to completely dismiss others' viewpoints or positions (the technical term is an argument, but I'll use statement instead). Identifying a fallacy just provides us a warning that the reason provided may not be enough to confirm or invalidate a statement and may lead to faulty conclusions. These are not unique to any group of people. With that said, let me start with the fallacy of fallacies.

The fallacy of fallacies. Just because a statement contains one or more fallacies doesn't mean the statement has a faulty conclusion.

What is true of the parts, then it's true of the whole, is **the fallacy of composition**.
Statement: *This book is terrible because the real estate section is terrible.*
Counter: *The real estate section is one section of +30 sections of this book. Therefore, does one chapter or segment define the whole book as terrible?*

If it's true of the whole, then it must be true of all the parts is the **fallacy of division**.
Statement: *Our Facebook group about supporting strong marriages receives great feedback without the topic of money conversations.*
Counter: *Supporting strong marriages includes many aspects. One crucial aspect - money conversations or how to discuss and make decisions with limited TEAM. resources — is an essential aspect of strong marriages. Without money conversations, there is a valuable component of strong marriages that is missing. Thus the Facebook page is well received AND could or would be*

received better with a component of money conversations. Those two statements can be correct at the same time.

They don't do as they say or "you too" is the **Tu quo que fallacy**.*
Statement: *My financial advisor told me to save 25% of my income, but he only saves 10%. Why should I listen to them?*
Counter: *Different people may have different circumstances; therefore, just because someone is not doing what they recommend – does not automatically invalidate their advice. The argument that the conclusion or recommendation is invalid because someone is not acting consistently with their argument falls into the Tu quo que fallacy.*

Multivariate causes condensed to one chosen variable **is a false dichotomy.***
Statement: *Why did you attend X.Y.Z. college?*
Reply: *I attended X.Y.Z. college because of the business school reputation, the alumni, the sports team, and the weather.*
Statement #2: *So you went to X.Y.Z. college **just because** of the weather.*

* common for many people.

Willfully misrepresenting an argument, often in an extreme way, is an example of a **Straw man.**
Statement: *Graduating from college leads to better jobs and income.*
Counter: *Bill Gates didn't graduate from college, and he was the wealthiest person in the world; therefore - I'm not going to college.*

Fallacious appeal to authority
Statement: *My father is an attorney, and he told me everything about investing.*

Counter: *Someone with expertise in law does not automatically make them an expert in the stock market or personal investment.*

If the counter relies upon how things have been historically done, then it may fall into the **appeal to tradition.**
Statement: *Money conversations are an important aspect of partnership finance.*
Counter: *If the topic was so important, why don't bookstores have a whole section of books dedicated to the subject partnership finance? Why does Google only contain a couple of articles on partnership finance? If we never addressed it before – why start now?*

The burden of Proof fallacy
Statement: *A book regarding partnership finance could be the most valuable wedding gift.*
Counter: *Prove it, and I'll believe it.*
We often make decisions with less than perfect information. Waiting for everything to align or perfectly tailored for you to make a decision can prove costly. By forcing the original person to prove an unprovable statement may fall into the Burden of Proof's fallacy.

Drawing a general conclusion from a biased or small sample size is the **Fallacy of Anecdotes.**
Statement: *I asked my cousin if they needed a book on money conversation, and they told me they have been married for over ten years, and they have no problems with money conversations.*
Counter: Married people will chuckle at this one. Anyone who states they have no problems with money conversations within their partnership may be focusing on conflict and discounting regular everyday financial decision making. Regarding the fallacy, asking one or two couples out of millions of couples is not a good representation of the population or poor sample size and could be considered anecdotal.

Asking a question with a built-in negative assumption. Any response that leads to someone appearing guilty is a **loaded question.**
Statement: *Why do you believe writing this book to show your old boss that you were talented was a good idea?*
Counter: *No good counter. A non-verbal look of "I'm not going to dignify that question with a response" can be provided.*

Two events happen in proximity, but there isn't a reason that one causes the other. **This is a False Cause Correlation.**
Statement: *The stock market goes higher when I go on vacation; therefore, we need to go on vacation next week.*
Counter: *Correlation does not equal causation.*

Denying the antecedent.
Statement: *Partnerships that make better decisions will be happier.*
Counter: *Are you saying that if partnerships are not happy; they didn't make the right decisions?*
They could be unhappy for other reasons – this is **denying the antecedent.**

Faulty analogy.
Statement: *Marriage is like a game of chess. In chess, you play to win. Therefore, in marriage, you are trying to win against your partner.*
Counter: *You can play to win against your partner, but this book is about working together with them to win or live better, given a certain amount of TEAM. resources.*

The slippery slope fallacy contends that one action will inevitably lead to another action, which will inevitably lead to another, which will inevitably lead to unfavorable results.

Statement: *If a wedding planner mention this money conversation book to a parent, then they will start recommending* *other finance and self-care books, and then they will need to make recommendations for everyone that solicits to them regarding newlyweds, and then they will be responsible for every recommendation.*

If any of these steps can be prevented, then it may fall into **the slippery slope fallacy**.

References

1. Age Wave (2018). *Women and Financial Wellness: Beyond the bottom line.* A Merrill Lynch Study conducted in partnership with Age Wage. https://agewave.com/what-we-do/landmark-research-and-consulting/research-studies/women-and-financial-wellness/

2. Alzheimer's Association. (n.d.). *Facts and figures.* Alzheimer's Association. Accessed 25 August 2020 at https://www.alz.org/alzheimers-dementia/facts-figures.

3. American Association for Long-Term Care Insurance. (n.d.) *Long-term care insurance health qualifications: Are you even eligible?* American Association for Long-Term Care Insurance. https://www.aaltci.org/long-term-care-insurance/learning-center/are-you-even-insurable.php.

4. The American Institute of Stress. (2019, October 21). *The good stress: How eustress helps you grow.* Daily Life. https://www.stress.org/the-good-stress-how-eustress-helps-you-grow.

5. American Psychological Association. (2018, October 30). *APA Stress in America™ survey: Generation Z stressed about issues in the news but least likely to vote.* American Psychological Association. https://www.apa.org/news/press/releases/2018/10/generation-z-stressed.

6. Balk, G (2018 September 15). *What is middle class in Seattle? Families now earn median of $121,000 Seattle Times.* https://www.seattletimes.com/seattle-news/data/what-is-middle-class-in-seattle-families-now-

earn-median-of-
121000/#:~:text=Families%20now%20earn%20median%
20of%20%24121%2C000,-
Originally%20published%20September&text=The%20me
dian%20income%20for%20a,in%20Seattle%20is%20now
%20%24161%2C000.

7. Benz, C. (2018, August 20). *75 must-know statistics about long-term care*. Morningstar.
    https://www.morningstar.com/articles/879494/75-must-know-statistics-about-long-term-care-2018-edition.

8. Bishop, P (2017). *College and Your Clients*
    https://www.paulabishop.com/

9. Certified Divorced Financial Analyst August 1 to 29, 2013 survey of 191 professionals from across North America, responded to the question: "According to what your divorcing clients have told you, what is the main reason that most of them are getting (or have gotten) divorced?" https://institutedfa.com/cdfa-professionals-reveal-leading-causes-of-divorce/.

10. Brinson, G, Beebower, G. Hood, L (1986). Determinants of Portfolio Performance Financial Analyst Journal.
    https://www.jstor.org/stable/4478947.

11. Center for Child Stress & Health. (n.d.) *What is toxic stress*. Center for Child Stress & Health, Florida State University College of Medicine.
    https://med.fsu.edu/childStress/whatis#:~:text=Tolerabl
    e%20Stress%3A%20%E2%80%9CA%20tolerable%20stres
    s,disaster%2C%20an%20act%20of%20terrorism.

12. Center on the Developing Child. (n.d.). *Toxic stress*. Center on the Developing Child, Harvard University.
    https://developingchild.harvard.edu/science/key-concepts/toxic-stress/#:~:text=Toxic%20stress%20response%20can%20o

ccur,hardship%E2%80%94without%20adequate%20adult%20support.

13. Congressional Budget Office. (2016). Detail of spending and enrollment for Medicaid for CBO's March 2016 baseline. https://www.cbo.gov/sites/default/files/recurringdata/51301-2016-03-medicaid.pdf.

14. Eisenberg, L. (Dec 2006). *The Number: What Do You Need for the Rest of Your Life, and What will Cost You. https://www.amazon.com/Number-What-Need-Rest-Your/dp/0743270320#ace-g2342880709.*

15. Family Caregiver Alliance. (n.d.). *Caregiver statistics: Demographics*. https://www.caregiver.org/caregiver-statistics-demographics.

16. Genworth. (2017). *Summary of 2017 survey findings*. Genworth. https://www.genworth.com/dam/Americas/US/PDFs/Consumer/corporate/cost-of-care/131168_081417.pdf.

17. Gutman, G. M. (n.d.). *A global look at the oldest-old and centenarians: Is it genes, diet, luck, or all combined?* American Society on Aging. https://www.asaging.org/blog/global-look-oldest-old-and-centenarians-it-genes-diet-luck-or-all-combined.

18. J. P. Morgan. (2020). Retirement insights. In *Guide to retirement 2020 edition*. https://am.jpmorgan.com/us/en/asset-management/gim/adv/insights/guide-to-retirement.

19. Kingsbury, K. B. (2017). *Breaking money silence: How to shatter money taboos, talk more openly about finances, and live a richer life*. Santa Barbara, CA: Praeger.

20. Klontz, K. (2009). Money Disorders are persistent, often rigid, patterns of self-destructive financial behaviors that cause significant stress, anxiety, emotional distress, and

impairment in major areas Retrieved from
https://books.google.com.pk/books?id=Brp_BAAAQBAJ&
pg=PA36&lpg=PA36&dq=Money+Disorders+are+persiste
nt,+often+rigid,+patterns+of+self-
destructive+financial+behaviors+that+cause+significant+
stress,+anxiety,+emotional+distress,+and+impairment+in
+major+areas+o (assessed on 26 August 2020).

21. Klontz, B. T., Britt, S. L., & Archuleta, K. L. (eds.). (2015). *Financial therapy: Theory, research, and practice*. Cham: Springer.

22. Lennick, D. & Jordan, K. (2011). *Financial intelligence: How to make smart, values-base decisions with your money and your life*. Minneapolis, MN: think2Perform.com.

23. Maslow, A. (1943). Psychological Review. *A Theory of Human Motivation. https://www.amazon.com/Theory-Human-Motivation-Abraham-Maslow/dp/1614274371.*

24. Markowitz, H.M. (March 1952). "Portfolio Selection". *The Journal of Finance*. **7** (1): 77–91. *doi:10.2307/2975974. JSTOR 2975974.*

25. Mehrabian, A. (1971). *Silent message*. Belmont, CA: Wadsworth Publishing.

26. National Foundation for Credit Counseling (NFCC) 2014 Prepared By: The Harris Poll Prepared For Consumer Financial Literacy 2014 Survey:

27. National Institute of Mental Health. (2018). *5 things you should know about stress*. National Institute of Mental Health. https://www.nimh.nih.gov/health/publications/stress/index.shtml

28. Nordman, E. C. (2016). *The state of long-term care insurance: The market, challenges and future innovations*. Kansas City, MO: National Association of

Insurance Commissioners Center for Insurance Policy and Research.

29. Northwestern Mutual. (2020). *The 2018 planning and progress study*. Northwestern Mutual. https://news.northwesternmutual.com/planning-and-progress-2018.Top of FormBottom of Form.

30. Pension Rights Center. (n.d.). *Income of today's older adults*. Pension Rights Center. http://www.pensionrights.org/publications/statistic/income-today%E2%80%99s-older-adults.

31. Shonkoff, J. P., Garner, A. S., Siegel, B. S., Dobbins, M. I., Earls, M. F., McGuinn, L., . . . Wood, D. L. (2012). *The lifelong effects of early childhood adversity and toxic stress. Pediatrics,* 129(1), e232-e246.

32. The Scan Foundation. (2013). *Who pays for long-term care in the US?* The Scan Foundation. https://www.thescanfoundation.org/sites/default/files/who_pays_for_ltc_us_jan_2013_fs.pdf

33. Thomas, H. P. (2013). *The mindful money mentality: How to find balance in your financial future*. St. Petersburg, FL: Porchview Publishing.

34. TutorialsPoint. (n.d.). *SCM-Performance measures*. TutorialsPoint. https://www.tutorialspoint.com/supply_chain_management/supply_chain_management_performance_measures.htm.

35. U.S. Bureau of Labor Statistics. (2018). *Fun facts about Millennials: Comparing expenditure patterns from the latest through the Greatest generation*. Monthly Labor Review. https://www.bls.gov/opub/mlr/2018/article/fun-facts-about-millennials.htm.

Think2perform <u>Behavioral Financial Advice program</u> BFA™ integrates traditional finance practices with psychology and neuroscience to improve emotional competency and decision-making behavior that increases effective usage of the financial plan for financial professionals and their clients.

The Certified Financial Planner CFP® designation is a professional certification mark for financial planners conferred by the Certified Financial Planner Board of Standards (CFP Board)® in the United States, and by 25 other organizations affiliated with Financial Planning Standards Board (FPSB), the owner of the CFP mark outside of the United States.
To receive authorization to use the designation, the candidate must meet education, examination, experience and ethics requirements, and pay an ongoing certification fee. The information relates specifically to CFP certification in the United States.

The Certified Investment Management Analyst® -CIMA® Certification is the only credential of its kind designed specifically for financial professionals seeking to distinguish themselves as advanced investment consultants. It requires successful completion of the educational component followed by a passing score on the CIMA® Certification Exam.

Any reference to the Certified Financial Planning CFP® in no way implies an endorsement or affiliation of any kind between Marriage & Money LLC and the CFP® program.

Acknowledgements

I want to thank so many people who contributed to this book including my professional and personal progression, because it's definitely been a journey. My family and especially my parents for supporting me despite my tendency to choose the more difficult path.

Jim Simmons & team of ICM Asset Management – you opened the door to investment management for me and I never looked back. To the two best managers - Patrick Schussman and Raleigh Peter's, both of you saw potential in me and took a chance. I may not fit in the "traditional" finance box but hopefully, this book indicates that I didn't fail you.

I want to acknowledge my mentors. Jim Davison and Leanne Strait Kramer. You've been so supportive – I'm not sure where I would be without you.

A grand acknowledgement to my Consulting Group family – you know who you are. My appreciation to the Smith Barney crew out of Tampa, FL – for accepting and adopting the left coast kid. To Michael Jancosek – I'm indebted to you for helping me transition from internal to external sales and getting me back to the west coast.

I want to thank Jim George, Katherine Roy, and J.P. Morgan Asset Management - I learned so much in such a short amount of time. You are a great organization, keep pushing the envelope. The members of think2Perform® for your content regarding behavioral financial advice. Keep evolving and shaping the industry.

Mike Hill and family for supporting me. Laura Humpf for our meetings/walks at Seward park. Jan Gullette for keeping me grounded. Matt Tillman – reliable sounding board and one of the most talented people I know. Dr. Whitney Blanco – who contributed when asked and conveniently pushed me to our grandmother's second favorite – well played. My brother-in law, Jason Moore – listening, understanding, and empathizing while separating as the #1 son-in law – respect.

I want to thank Brianna Grantham of BJG Consulting for her early marketing support. Mike Plaster of Plaster Consulting for his editing and guidance through this whole process. Nora Luviksen of TheTable Mediation for early contributions regarding conflict resolution and mediation. David Innes – you are a wealth of information related to technology. To all my former financial planning clients – for trusting me with your dreams and finances. The team of editors: Beth Tyler, Laurie Austin, Christina Sarich, Porsche Steele, Julie Anne Gniadek, Cortni Merritt, Neil Mathews, Amanda Noonan, Erika Nelson, Coralie Emberson, Autumn Knowlton. And other contributors: Mike Miller, Kevin Neynaber, Mack McCoy, Nguire Taylor, Sally Li, and Matt Reese.

And finally but definitely not least, Mr. Three Feet High & Rising and Mr. Me Too for providing constant laughs, lessons, and motivation. Daddy loves you.

About the Author

Roderick M. Givens, CFP®, CIMA®, BFA™

Is a financial creative with a diverse background since 1998 in the fields of financial planning, business development, asset management, and wealth management. He's held positions as an investment analyst, manager, business development director, business loan officer, investment sales director, and financial planner at Smith Barney, Morgan Stanley, William Blair & Co., J.P. Morgan, and the Rainier Valley Community Development Fund. In 2015, he founded a Registered Investment Advisory (RIA) firm in the state of Washington: RainierView Advisors LLC. And in 2018, he founded Marriage & Money LLC a firm focused on financial education for partnerships. He has served on non-profit boards of his local community club, chambers of commerce, community development fund.

This money conversations book represents an integration of his professional and personal experience as a husband, father, and community member regarding finance, behavioral psychology, and sociology.

He calls the Rainier Beach area of Seattle, WA home.

If you are looking for my wealth
Search for memories and good times
Delivered through God's messenger
Stored deep in Solomon's mines.